PRESIDENTS
AT WAR

HOW
FRANKLIN D.
ROOSEVELT
FOUGHT
WORLD WAR II

Earle Rice Jr.

Enslow Publishing
101 W. 23rd Street
Suite 240
New York, NY 10011
USA

enslow.com

Published in 2018 by Enslow Publishing, LLC.
101 W. 23rd Street, Suite 240, New York, NY 10011

Library of Congress Cataloging-in-Publication Data

Names: Rice, Earle, author.
  Title: How Franklin D. Roosevelt fought World War II / Earle Rice Jr.
  Description: New York : Enslow Publishing, 2018. | Series: Presidents at war |
    Includes bibliographical references and index. | Audience: Grades 7-12.
  Identifiers: LCCN 2017004612 | ISBN 9780766085275 (library bound)
  Subjects: LCSH: Roosevelt, Franklin D. (Franklin Delano), 1882–1945—Juvenile
    literature. | Presidents—United States—Biography—Juvenile literature. | United
    States—Politics and government—1933–1945—Juvenile literature. | World War,
    1939-1945—United States—Juvenile literature.
  Classification: LCC E807 .R49 2017 | DDC 973.917092—dc23
  LC record available at https://lccn.loc.gov/2017004612

Printed in the United States of America

To Our Readers: We have done our best to make sure all website addresses in this
book were active and appropriate when we went to press. However, the author and the
publisher have no control over and assume no liability for the material available on those
websites or on any websites they may link to. Any comments or suggestions can be sent by
email to customerservice@enslow.com.

Photo Credits: Cover, pp. 1, 5, 8, 19, 30, 42, 52, 63, 73, 84, 94, 104, 113 (FDR) Franklin
D. Roosevelt Presidential Library & Museum; cover, p. 1 (Battle) National Archives; p. 4
Archive Photos/Getty Images; p. 9 Fine Art/Corbis Historical/Getty Images; p. 10
Chronicle/Alamy Stock Photo; p. 12 Pintai Suchachaisri/Moment/Getty Images; pp. 15,
23, 79, 96 Keystone/Hulton Archive/Getty Images; pp. 17, 20, 31, 56, 58, 64, 68, 69, 105,
108 Bettmann/Getty Images; p. 22 Heinrich Hoffmann/Archive Photos/Getty Images;
pp. 24, 34, 36, 45, 74, 89 © AP Images; p. 26 Shadowxfox/Wikimedia; p. 32 Jack Wilkes/
The LIFE Picture Collection/Getty Images; p. 38 Fox Photos/Hulton Archive/Getty
Images; pp. 43, 50 Hulton Archive/Getty Images; p. 48 FPG/Archive Photos/Getty
Images; p. 53 war posters/Alamy Stock Photo; pp. 55, 112 Hulton Deutsch/Corbis
Historical/Getty Images; p. 61 Serge Plantureux/Corbis Historical/Getty Images; p. 76
Roger Viollet/Getty Images; p. 80 Keystone Features/Hulton Archive/Getty Images;
p. 82 PhotoQuest/Archive Photos/Getty Images; p. 85 ullstein bild/Getty Images; p. 87
Keystone-France/Gamma-Keystone/Getty Images; p. 90 Jeffrey Markowitz/Sygma/
Getty Images; pp. 93, 114 Corbis Historical/Getty Images; p. 95 Galerie Bilderwelt/
Hulton Archive/Getty Images; p. 101 PJF Military Collection/Alamy Stock Photo; p. 102
David E. Scherman/The LIFE Picture Collection/Getty Images; p. 106 John Stevenson/
Corbis Historical/Getty Images.

★ CONTENTS ★

INTRODUCTION 5

CHAPTER 1   DATE OF INFAMY 8

CHAPTER 2   PATH TOWARD DISASTER 19

CHAPTER 3   THE WINDS OF WAR 30

CHAPTER 4   AMERICA'S UNDECLARED WAR 42

CHAPTER 5   AMERICA JOINS THE FIGHT 52

CHAPTER 6   A WORLD AT WAR 63

CHAPTER 7   TURNING THE TIDE 73

CHAPTER 8   TRIUMPH AND TRAGEDY 84

CHAPTER 9   ENDGAME IN THE PACIFIC 94

CHAPTER 10   "RAIN OF RUIN" 104

CONCLUSION 113

CHRONOLOGY   116

CHAPTER NOTES   119

GLOSSARY   124

FURTHER READING   125

INDEX   126

Young Franklin is age eleven in this portrait, where he is shown holding hands with his mother, Sara Delano Roosevelt.

INTRODUCTION

Franklin Delano Roosevelt—a man destined to guide the free world through its most devastating conflict—entered a world of privilege in the Hudson Valley town of Hyde Park, New York, on January 30, 1882.

Born into a wealthy old-Dutch family from Dutchess County, New York, Roosevelt—widely known as "FDR"—was educated at Groton School and Harvard College in Massachusetts. At Groton, he ranked fourth in a class of nineteen. He graduated in the spring of 1900. FDR excelled in extracurricular activities while at Harvard but maintained only average grades. The future world leader graduated with a bachelor of arts degree in history in 1903.

While still in college, FDR began courting Anna Eleanor Roosevelt, his fifth cousin once removed. She was the niece of their mutual uncle, Theodore Roosevelt, the twenty-sixth president of the United States. Franklin married Eleanor in 1905. Their union produced six children, a daughter and five sons, one of whom died in infancy. Over time, they drifted apart. They remained married but detached.

Roosevelt entered Columbia Law School in New York City in 1904 but dropped out after passing the New York State bar examination in 1907. He soon embarked on a career of public service. In 1910, he ran for, and was elected to, the New York State Senate. En route to high office, he subsequently served as assistant secretary of the Navy in World War I. FDR was later elected governor of New York in 1929.

In 1932, despite a polio-induced paralysis from the waist down at the age of thirty-nine, FDR reached the pinnacle of American politics with his election as president of the United States. He assumed the office and its burdens amid depression at home and discontent abroad. The collapse of Wall Street in 1929 had undermined the American economy. Millions of workers lost their jobs, homes, and savings in the Great Depression that followed. Economic and political unrest abroad posed a further threat to the stability of the American way of life.

At his inauguration address, Roosevelt set about immediately to calm the collective apprehension of all Americans at a turning point in world history. In his silvery oratorical style, he offered assurance that the nation was in steady hands. "[F]irst of all, let me assert my firm belief," he said, "that the only thing we have to fear is fear itself."[1] He spoke for fifteen minutes and instilled confidence in a nation desperate for leadership.

Throughout the 1930s, Roosevelt worked tirelessly to heal America's wounded economy, passing monumental legislation under the umbrellas of the "New Deal" and the "Second New Deal." As war clouds gathered abroad, he artfully maneuvered US foreign policy to maintain

American neutrality, while concurrently preparing his nation for war.

During those tumultuous years, FDR formed a friendship and high regard for Great Britain's prime minister Winston Churchill. Together, they forged an alliance—later joined by Premier Joseph Stalin of the Soviet Union (USSR)—that would defeat Germany and Japan and restore order in the postwar world.

CHAPTER ONE

DATE OF INFAMY

America's entry into World War II began on a tranquil Sunday morning at a faraway setting in the mid-Pacific Ocean. It began on a small island that had been—up till then—a paradise of sorts, basking in warm sunlight and cooled by fragrant breezes. It began at precisely 7:55 a.m. At that moment, a wave of Japanese aircraft appeared over Oahu in the Hawaiian Islands and launched a surprise attack on the US naval base at Pearl Harbor and other US military installations on the island. Over the next two hours, the lives of all Americans would be forever altered. It was December 7, 1941.

Twelve days earlier, at dawn on November 26 (Japan time), ships of Japan's First Air Fleet put to sea out of Hitokappu Bay (now Kasatka Bay) in Itorofu (now Iturup), one of the Kuril Islands. The fleet—also called *Kido Butai* (Striking Force)—sailed under the command of Admiral Chuichi Nagumo of the Imperial Japanese Navy (IJN).

Once clear of Hitokappu, Nagumo set a northern course and plowed into the choppy seas of the mist-and-fog-

The US destroyer *Shaw* erupts in a billowing array of flame and smoke after Japanese bombs strike its ordnance and touch off a devastating explosion.

shrouded North Pacific where commercial vessels seldom ventured. En route to his assigned destination, he would have many lonely hours to ponder his final instructions from Admiral Isoroku Yamamoto, commander in chief of the Japanese Combined Fleet: "In case negotiations with the United States reach a successful conclusion, the task force will immediately put about and return to the homeland."[1]

Kido Butai

Admiral Nagumo assembled a formidable striking force known as the *Kido Butai*. The final formation of his fleet and the roles of each of its elements were

- Six large aircraft carriers—*Akagi, Kaga, Hiryu, Soryu, Zuikaku,* and *Shokaku*—along with their 423 aircraft, formed the nucleus of the attack force.
- Two battleships—*Hiei* and *Kirishima*—and two heavy cruisers—*Tone* and *Chikuma*—provided heavy firepower as backup against the unexpected.
- Nine destroyers and one light cruiser—*Abukuma*—provided protective screening.
- Three submarines patrolled the waters forward and abreast of the main body of the fleet.

Zero fighter aircraft prepare to launch from the Japanese carrier *Akagi*.

Seven days later, on December 2—while Japan's emissaries spoke of peace with US officials in Washington, DC—Admiral Nagumo received a coded radio message from Admiral Yamamoto. The message read: "*Niitaka yama nobore ichi-ni-rei-ya*," Japanese for "Climb Mount Niitaka, 1208."[2] These were code words calling for the attack on Pearl Harbor to proceed on December 8 (Sunday, December 7, US time). The fleet was then some 940 miles (1,513 kilometers) due north of Midway Island.

At 1130 on December 6, the First Air Fleet swung about, corrected course to 180 degrees due south toward Hawaii, and advanced speed to twenty knots. Ten minutes later, Admiral Nagumo ordered the historic Z flag hoisted on *Akagi*, his flagship carrier. The flag was the same one raised by Admiral Tōgō after defeating the Russian fleet in the naval Battle of Tsushima in the Russo-Japanese War of 1904–1905. It symbolized victory. Nagumo then signaled a message from Yamamoto to the rest of the fleet: "The rise and fall of the Empire depends upon this battle. Every man will do his duty."[3] Cheers rang out across the *Kido Butai*.

Japanese strategists had planned the attack for a Sunday for good reason: after weekday training exercises at sea, the American fleet anchored in at the naval base on weekends and observed a relaxed routine. Japan's war planners falsely expected to find four aircraft carriers at berth on the day of the attack. A last-minute message relayed from Tokyo, from an espionage source in Hawaii, reported that all eight battleships of the US Pacific Fleet were in the harbor—but no carriers. No one among the Air Fleet felt more disappointed than Commander Mitsuo Fuchida, the designated leader of the impending air attack on Pearl Harbor.

Mount Niitaka

Mount Niitaka (now Yushan) was the highest peak in the Japanese Empire. Yamamoto's message symbolized the mountainous task that faced Japan and its First Air Fleet: Yamamoto, who had spent time in America, knew that the defeat of the United States would come only after a long, steep climb—if at all.

Mount Yushan, Taiwan, formerly known as Mount Niitaka, viewed from the mountain's main peak.

"The U.S. battleships, though secondary to the carriers, were still considered an important target," Fuchida wrote later, "and there was also a faint possibility that some of the American carriers might have returned to Pearl Harbor by the time our planes struck."[4] Admiral Nagumo's fleet, now closing fast on its Hawaiian destination, steamed on through the night.

Tora! Tora! Tora!

Commander Fuchida arose aboard the *Akagi* at 0500 on Sunday, December 7, 1941—the date of the attack designated as X-Day. After a celebratory breakfast of rice and red snapper with his pilots, he went on to the operations room for a sake toast and final briefing. "On the blackboard was written the positions of ships in Pearl Harbor as of 0600 December 7," he recalled later. "We were 230 miles [370 km] due north of Oahu."[5]

During the final briefings, at 0550, six aircraft carriers and their escorts turned almost due east into a brisk wind and prepared to launch, pitching violently in heavy seas. Pilots soon rushed on deck and scrambled to their planes. Aircraft engines roared to life, and carrier deck plates vibrated. After a weather delay of twenty minutes, a green lamp waved in a circle to signal "Take off!" Fighter planes began their short runs and lifted off. High-level bombers followed, then dive bombers, and lastly torpedo bombers—183 aircraft in all. "After circling over the fleet formation," Commander Mitsuo Fuchida noted, "we set course due south for Pearl Harbor. The time was 6:15 a.m."[6]

For the next hour and forty minutes, Fuchida led the First Air Fleet's first wave of attackers on an undetected flight toward its destination of devastation. As time passed, his eyes strained for the sight of land. Suddenly, through an opening in the cloud cover, he glimpsed a long white line of surf breaking against the shore directly below him—*Oahu!*

Veering right, Fuchida guided his pilots westward toward Pearl Harbor. A morning mist was rising over the Oahu plain, but the sky was clear over their target. Using binoculars from somewhere off Lahilahi Point, he counted seven battleships riding at anchor in the harbor, but no carriers. He did not see *Pennsylvania* in dry dock across the channel. At 0749, Fuchida ordered his radio operator to send the Attack! command to all pilots. His operator complied at once, tapping out the preset code signal *To, to, to*—the first syllable of *totsugekiseyo*, Japanese for "charge."

Seconds later, as his torpedo bombers swept in across Battleship Row, at the southeast end of Ford Island, Fuchida ordered his radioman to tap out *Tora! Tora! Tora!* (Tiger! Tiger! Tiger!). It was a signal that would inform the entire Japanese navy that the first attack wave had caught the Pacific Fleet by complete surprise.

Wholesale Destruction

The first-wave attackers split into four groups and roared in on their preassigned targets. Primary targets consisted of the Army's Schofield Barracks and airfields at Wheeler, Hickam, Bellows, and Mokuleia; Marine Corps air stations at Ewa and Kaneohe Bay; the Naval Air Station at Ford Island; and the seven battlewagons anchored along Battleship Row—*Arizona, Tennessee, Maryland, California, Nevada, West Virginia*, and *Oklahoma*—plus *Pennsylvania* in dry dock. Other warships anchored in the harbor provided targets of opportunity.

Six minutes after Fuchida's *To* signal, bombs began to fall at Pearl Harbor. Low-flying "Kate" torpedo bombers swept across Battleship Row and opened gaping holes below the waterlines of four battlewagons. "Val" dive bombers followed, tearing up steel decks and demolishing gun turrets and superstructures. Other Kates doubled as

The Aichi D3A2 ("Val"), premier dive bomber of the Imperial Japanese Navy, was instrumental in crippling the US fleet at Pearl Harbor.

high-level bombers to add finishing touches to the wholesale destruction of the US Pacific Fleet.

Arizona took a torpedo and eight bombs. It erupted in a massive explosion and sank, killing almost a thousand men. Five more torpedoes tore into *Oklahoma*. She turned over and sank, trapping her remaining crew below decks. *California* absorbed two torpedoes and a bomb. *Nevada* made a run for the open sea but beached at Hospital Point after taking a torpedo and six bomb hits. Six torpedoes and a bomb struck *West Virginia*, partially sinking her. *Maryland*, *Tennessee*, and *Pennsylvania* escaped relatively lightly, each sustaining two bomb hits. *Utah*, an obsolete battlewagon used as a target ship, took two torpedo hits on the west side of Ford Island. She also sank.

Among the thirty-eight cruisers and destroyers also in harbor, eight of them took damage but lived to fight again. Several smaller vessels were also damaged or sunk.

While Pearl Harbor was erupting in flame, smoke, and thunderous explosions, other first-wave attackers were inflicting similar destruction on the island's airfields. A second wave of 167 bombers and fighters led by Lieutenant Commander Shigekazu Shimazaki arrived over Oahu about 0840, but the first wave had already done most of the damage. "Zeke" fighters and Val bombers destroyed 188 American aircraft and damaged another 159, most of them on the ground.

Countless episodes of American heroism wrote the story of Japan's treacherous attack. The actions of Chief Aviation Ordnanceman John Finn at Kaneohe typified the American response. Finn leaped from bed and rushed to the air station to set up a machine gun in one of the hangars. His Medal of Honor citation tells it all: "Although painfully wounded many times, he continued to man his gun and to return the enemy's fire vigorously, and with telling effect throughout the enemy strafing and bombing attacks, and with complete disregard for his own personal safety."[7]

American casualties totaled 2,403 dead and 1,178 wounded. Japanese casualties were comparatively light. Only twenty-nine of their aircraft failed to make it back to their carriers—less than 10 percent of their attacking force.

War Declared

On December 8, 1941, US President Franklin Delano Roosevelt—routinely identified by his initials "FDR"—addressed a joint session of Congress. He announced the surprise Japanese naval and air attack on Pearl Harbor and described December 7 as "a date which will live in infamy."

Following the Japanese surprise attack on Pearl Harbor on December 7, 1941, President Franklin D. Roosevelt addresses a joint session of Congress to request a formal declaration of war against Japan.

Because of this "unprovoked and dastardly attack,"[8] he asked Congress to declare war against Japan.

In less than an hour, Congress complied: the US Senate unanimously approved the declaration 82-0; the House of Representatives supported the measure 388-1. Montana Republican Jeannette Rankin—a lifelong pacifist who also voted against a declaration of war on Germany in

World War I—cast the lone dissenting vote. Her vote was recorded as *present*.

Three days later, on December 11, 1941, Germany and Italy declared war on the United States. Americans—led by a man bound to a wheelchair, but hardly handi-capped—answered the call to arms and joined history's most destructive war.

PATH TOWARD DISASTER

Franklin D. Roosevelt took office as the thirty-second president of the United States at a time of extreme economic challenges at home. Americans elected him on the promise of hope and recovery. Through sweeping reform legislation—proposed by him and enacted by Congress—he lifted the spirits of a depressed nation and met the challenges head-on.

While FDR struggled to restore jobs and revitalize businesses and agriculture at home, the seeds of political discontent were taking root abroad. Even greater challenges loomed just over the horizon for the American president— challenges that would dismay many lesser men. But life has a way of allotting great challenges to great men.

In Europe, Germany stood in the throes of a slow recovery from the harsh reparations imposed upon it by the Treaty of Versailles that ended World War I. Adolf Hitler and the Nazis—an acronym for *Nationalsozialists* (National Socialists)—were rising to power. Hitler promised to restore Germany's former greatness and expand its living

Troops of Hitler's Schutzstaffel, or SS (Elite Guard), march en masse into Prague to enforce martial law after the execution of three Czech rebels.

space (*Lebensraum*). He was named chancellor of Germany in 1933 and set out to make good on his promises.

On October 14, 1933, Germany resigned from the League of Nations, a peacekeeping organization formed by the victorious Allied nations after World War I. In violation of the Treaty of Versailles, Hitler began to rearm Germany under the very noses of the world at large. In Britain, only Lord of the Admiralty Winston Churchill seemed to notice: "I look with wonder at our thoughtless crowds disporting themselves in the summer sunshine," while across the North Sea, "a terrible process is astir. *Germany is arming.*"[1]

Hitler's rearmament program continued secretly for the next two years. By 1935, the size of his army had tripled to 300,000 troops. A compulsory military draft was set to deliver 250,000 more. His formidable air force boasted some 2,500 war planes. Minister of Aviation Hermann Göring conducted pilot training under the guise of the League for Air Sports. Surface and undersea forces grew at an explosive rate. Submarines were secretly built in Finland, the Netherlands, and Spain. Britain, France, and Italy protested German rearmament but did little about it.

Incursion and Civil War

At the same time, the forces of Italian dictator Benito Mussolini, Mr. Fascist himself, invaded Abyssinia (now Ethiopia) in October 1935. Mussolini held grandiose notions of reestablishing the Roman Empire. He used a border incident between Italian Somaliland (now Somalia) and Abyssinia as an excuse to invade the latter nation. In reality, Mussolini acted in a manner influenced by Hitler's pursuit of "living space." He saw Abyssinia as an opportunity to

Adolf Hitler

Adolf Hitler, born in Austria in 1889, served in the German army in World War I. He was wounded and gassed, decorated for bravery, and discharged as a corporal. Hitler felt that the German army had not lost the war but had been betrayed by civilians on the home front with a "stab in the back." His bitterness led him into politics. He became a founding member of the Nazi Party.

After a failed coup to take over the German government, known as the Beer Hall Putsch, and nine months in prison, he rose to power through the ballot box. As chancellor of Germany and head of the Nazi Party, he adopted the title of *Führer* (leader) and cemented his dictatorial authority. His quest for "living space" and world domination ignited World War II.

Adolf Hitler, future chancellor and dictator of Nazi Germany, salutes his followers in Munich in the spring of 1932.

Benito Mussolini

Benito Mussolini, Italy's future dictator, was born in 1883, the son of a blacksmith. He was an ardent socialist in his youth and edited the party newspaper *Avanti!* (Forward!). After serving in the Italian army (1915–1917), he returned to civilian life as editor of *Il Popolo d'Italia* (The People of Italy). In 1919, he formed a political group that marked the beginning of Fascism.

After leading a march on Rome that toppled the Italian government in 1922, Mussolini established the Fascists as the majority political party. He became known as "Il Duce," meaning "the chief" in Italian. In 1936, he formed an alliance with Hitler that gave birth to the Axis powers.

Italian dictator Benito Mussolini salutes a throng of followers during a public address in Rome.

provide land for unemployed Italians. Nor did the chance to acquire Abyssinia's mineral resources go unnoticed by the Italian dictator.

Abyssinian warriors faced off against Italian forces, pitting spears against tanks and planes. Il Duce's son Vittorio waxed poetically about an air attack in the six-month war that lacked not for atrocities: "One group of horsemen gave me the impression of a budding rose unfolding as the bomb fell in their midst and blew them up."[2] Italy's quick victory over its overmatched foe surprised no one.

The following year, General Francisco Franco mounted a military revolt against the Republican government of Spain in 1936, igniting a bloody civil war. Hitler and

American Friends of Spanish Democracy and one of their ambulances in Paris before leaving for Spain in March 1937.

Abraham Lincoln Brigade

American volunteers in Spain formed several battalions known as the Abraham Lincoln Brigade. They served largely in medical and transportation capacities. Spain's Civil War (1936–1939) claimed the lives of about 500,000 victims; of the 2,800 American volunteers, about one-third died in Spain.

Mussolini, along with Joseph Stalin, premier of the Soviet Union (USSR), seized the opportunity to train their armed forces in a real war. Germany and Italy sent men and arms to Franco; the USSR supported government Loyalists.

Some 2,800 American volunteers formed the Abraham Lincoln Brigade and fought against Franco's Fascist forces. A loophole in US neutrality laws allowed American companies to sell various commodities to Franco during Spain's Civil War (1936–1939). By the end of 1939, Franco owed these companies—Standard Oil, Ford, General Motors, and others—more than $100 million.

American sympathies generally lay with the Loyalists. But most Americans were suffering in their own right from the effects of the Depression. Few wanted the US government to get involved with foreign conflicts. FDR seemed to share their desire to remain uninvolved. Soon after the start of the war in Spain, in a speech to a public gathering in Chautauqua, New York, he said, "I have seen war. I have seen blood running from the wounded … I have seen children starving … I hate war."[3]

Though FDR had not experienced combat firsthand, he had toured Europe during World War I as assistant secretary of the Navy. He cautioned would-be aggressors that the American conscience rebelled against war and that those nations who provoked war would lose the sympathy of all Americans.

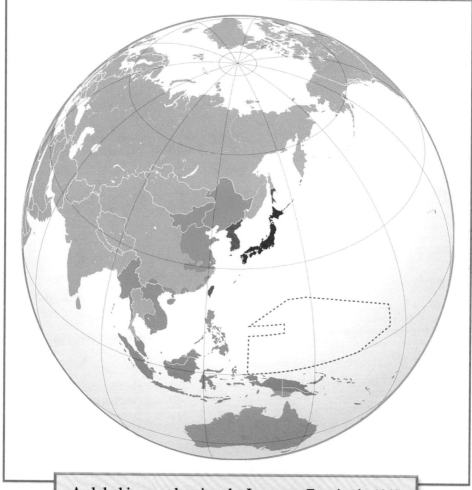

A global image showing the Japanese Empire in 1942.

Asian Dominance

Meanwhile, at the other side of the world, Japanese leaders were well on the way to developing a master plan to dominate Southeast Asia and the islands of the western half of the Pacific. Named the Greater East Asia Co-Prosperity Sphere, the territory stretched from the Kuril Islands southeast to the Marshall Islands, west to the Dutch East Indies (now Republic of Indonesia), and formed a sweeping curve to India.

Japan began its quest for Asian dominance by invading and occupying Manchuria. There they created the puppet state of Manchukuo in 1931. The League of Nations condemned Japan's actions and called for Manchuria to be returned to China.

Japan answered by withdrawing its membership in 1933 and tightening its grasp on Manchuria. Japanese leaders defended their aggression, citing an Asian-style Monroe Doctrine. In essence, it advocated Japan's right to dominate East Asia, much like the United States held sway over the Americas. Other countries should keep out of Asia, it asserted, just as other countries generally kept out of the Western Hemisphere.

As storm clouds gathered abroad, Americans remained largely isolationist at first. Congress stood firmly opposed to foreign entanglements. But as Germany and Japan continued down avenues of aggression, Americans started to sympathize with victims of Fascist belligerence. The public debate over nonintervention heightened. Continuing aggressions abroad gave rise to the Neutrality Acts of the 1930s. They were enacted to curb any further American involvement in foreign affairs.

Neutrality Acts

In the 1930s, Congress enacted a series of laws that specifically stated the terms of US neutrality. Inspired by a lingering public dissatisfaction with the loss of American blood and treasure in World War I, they were designed to keep the United States out of future foreign wars. Many Americans felt that the so-called War to End All Wars was driven by the interests of bankers and munitions traders who profited from the war. This thinking fueled a growing "isolationist" movement in America. Its supporters argued that the United States should give a wide berth to future wars and stay clear of financial deals with warring nations.

Congress passed the Neutrality Act of 1935 in August of that year in reaction to growing fears of a major war in Europe. In the event of war, it prohibited the sale of "arms, ammunition, and implements of war"[4] to aggressor nations. It also advised Americans traveling in war zones to do so at their own risk. FDR questioned the meaning of "implements of war" and who determined whether a state of war existed.

FDR thought about vetoing the measure, but he finally relented after the bill was rewritten to give the president executive power over the items in question. He really did not want his foreign policy decisions to be constrained by legislative actions, but he chose not to challenge public sentiment and congressional opinion. Reluctantly, he signed the measure.

"I have approved this Joint Resolution because it was intended as an expression of the fixed desire of the Government and the people of the United States to avoid any action which might involve us in war," FDR said.[5]

But he added that changing conditions might demand a new approach. "History," he said, "is filled with unforeseeable situations that call for some flexibility of action."[6]

Congress extended the act to May 1937, further prohibiting Americans from making loans to warring nations. Public concern over the rise of European Fascism and the outbreak of war in Spain lent further support to the Neutrality Act of 1937. The act empowered the president to forbid US citizens from traveling on ships of belligerents; to prevent US merchant ships from transporting arms to nations at war; and to force belligerents to pay for goods before shipment, a provision popularly known as "cash and carry." No longer would American companies be left holding the bag for unpaid deliveries as was the case in Spain's civil war. In time, more Neutrality Acts would follow.

For the time being, Americans were content to reside safely behind the great watery barrier formed by the Atlantic Ocean—while the world around them marched inexorably down a path toward disaster.

THE WINDS OF WAR

$\mathbf{D}$uring FDR's second term (1937–1941), the drumbeat of Fascism resonated louder than ever in Europe, and the winds of war blew stronger in the Far East. The belligerent machinations of Hitler and Mussolini in Europe, along with Japan's increasing aggressions against China in Asia, threatened world stability and peace. In the face of growing resistance from isolationists, FDR started to focus less on domestic issues and more on foreign policy matters. His eyes soon turned toward the Far East.

Undeclared War in China

In China, Japanese and Chinese forces clashed at the Marco Polo Bridge on July 7, 1937. The bridge stands at a rail junction at Wanping (now Lugouqiao), about nine miles (15 kilometers) southwest of Peiping (now Beijing). Named for the first Western traveler to cross over it in the thirteenth century, its thirty graceful arches span the Yongding River. Recent Japanese troop maneuvers in the area had already caused tension among members of the Chinese garrison stationed there.

Benito Mussolini and Adolf Hitler review a Nazi
parade staged in honor of Il Duce's visit to Germany.

Reportedly, a Japanese soldier had gone missing. In the
ensuing search for him, a Japanese lieutenant marched his
troops over the bridge and straight to the gates of town.
He demanded to search the garrison for his missing soldier.
The commander of the Chinese garrison refused his
demand. At 11:30 p.m., several shots rang out, shattering
the stillness of the warm summer evening. Fighting began

Two Nationalist Chinese soldiers gaze at the Yongding River from the wall of the Marco Polo (or Lugou) Bridge outside Peking (now Beijing) in December 1945. An incident at the bridge in July 1937 touched off the Second Sino-Japanese War.

and soon escalated, touching off what the Japanese refer to as the "China Incident." The Chinese call it the "war of resistance." In either case, the fighting quickly spread to central China. The two nations plunged into the Second Sino-Japanese War (1937–1945), which eventually merged into World War II.

The fighting moved south in August 1937. Japanese soldiers struck Shanghai. They chased the retreating Chinese up the Yangtze valley to the then Nationalist Chinese capital of Nanking (now Nanjing). In December, the Japanese assaulted the city and unleashed a six-week-long reign of terror—shootings, bayonetings, beheadings, and rapes—that took the lives of an estimated forty thousand victims. The scourge became known as the infamous "Rape of Nanking."

Another "incident" that occurred in conjunction with the terror of Nanking struck closer to home for angry Americans. On December 12, Japanese bombers intentionally bombed and sank the US shallow-draft gunboat *Panay* upstream from Nanking, while it was evacuating American nationals from the fighting zone. FDR sent a strong message to the Japanese, demanding an apology and reparations. Some American officials viewed Japan's action as a warning to the United States to stay out of its fight with China. But the Japanese met FDR's demands, and the matter was quickly consigned to the history books.

Despite the ire of most Americans, they still held strong isolationist feelings, as did the US Congress. There was little else that FDR could do at the time. But he explored the possibility of seizing Japanese assets—outside the law, if necessary—as another way of controlling Japan's

In an unprovoked attack, Japanese bombers bombed and sank the US gunboat *Panay* in the Yangtze River near Shanghai, China, on December 12, 1937.

aggressive conduct. "After all," he told his cabinet, "if Italy and Japan have evolved a technique of fighting without declaring war, why can't we develop a similar one?"[1]

Quarantine

In a speech delivered in Chicago on October 5, 1937, FDR called for a "quarantine" against aggressor nations. Though he did not name the aggressors, his words contained an ill-concealed reference to Germany, Italy, and Japan. In his eloquent speaking style, FDR cautioned against unchecked international lawlessness. He warned: "Let no one imagine that America will escape, that America may expect mercy, that this Western Hemisphere will not be attacked."[2]

His speech compared war with disease and isolation of aggressor nations with the quarantining of patients. FDR failed to specifically define "quarantine," but it was generally thought to mean economic sanctions and diplomatic isolation. His vagueness allowed him to avoid commitment to any specific policy. He emphasized the importance of honoring international treaties as a means of ensuring world peace.

Cash and Carry

The "cash and carry" provision of the Neutrality Act of 1937 authorized the sale of commodities to belligerent nations in Europe in return for immediate cash payment and transport by the recipients. FDR believed this provision would benefit France and Great Britain in the event of war since they controlled the seas. He chose not to invoke the "cash and carry" requirement against China, however, because China could afford the cost of arms imports in its war with Japan. Isolationists protested. They claimed his maneuver undermined US neutrality. FDR shunned their criticism, and his neutral foreign policy gradually shifted to one more directed toward countering aggressors.

On October 5, 1937, at the dedication of Chicago's Outer Drive Highway Bridge, FDR waves to a crowd of three-quarters of a million and pleads for peace in an increasingly belligerent world.

Dealing With Gangsters

On September 7, 1937, Hitler declared the end of the Treaty of Versailles (which ended World War I and imposed heavy reparations on Germany). German troops subsequently tramped across the border into Austria in March 1938. In an action known as *Anschluss* (union) and described as the political union of Germany and Austria, Hitler annexed the land of his birth. He justified his action under the Nazi slogan *"Ein Volk, ein Reich, ein* Führer."[3] The slogan

Short of War

FDR's "quarantine" speech received mixed reviews. Some critics felt it would lend further support to American isolationism. Others feared it might brand Americans as the "world's policemen." When the public showed little enthusiasm for his speech, FDR refrained from introducing any new foreign policy measures at that time. But to shrewd observers, the speech signaled FDR's intention to shift the traditional US nonintervention policy to one of increasing aggressiveness—but one short of war itself.

("one people, one empire, one leader") ignited a wave of ultra-nationalism in Germany and moved Europe closer to war.

The League of Nations, the Catholic Church, and the British government headed by Prime Minister Neville Chamberlain passively accepted Hitler's Austrian annexation. At that time, the British still viewed Hitler as a protective buffer against Communism. In light of European passivity, FDR felt it would be unwise to protest the annexation and stir up American emotions to no good end. But he privately abhorred Chamberlain's seeming eagerness to placate the German dictator.

In a press conference on March 11, 1938, FDR commented on Chamberlain's acquiescence guardedly: "If a Chief of Police makes a deal with the leading gangsters and the deal results in no more hold-ups, that Chief of

"Feeding the Crocodile"

Britain's Chamberlain-led government further aggravated FDR when it formally recognized Italy's conquest of Abyssinia in April. Chamberlain hoped to slake Il Duce's thirst for empire, while stabilizing Britain's Mediterranean route to the Suez Canal and India beyond. FDR viewed such recognition as a reward for belligerent behavior. He worried about the adverse effect it might have on Japanese aggressions in the Far East "and upon the nature of the peace terms Japan may demand of China."[4] Looking on as a distant observer, Winston Churchill felt that Chamberlain and his cabinet were "feeding the crocodiles."[5] And the Nazi crocodile was hungry.

A trio of British Royal Air Force fighters overfly a transport in the Suez Canal in March 1938.

Police will be called a great man—but if the gangsters do not live up to their word the Chief of Police will go to jail."[6]

"Peace for Our Time"

In September 1938, Hitler's insatiable hunger for more "living space" led him next to the Sudetenland. The Sudetenland was a small area in Bohemia adjacent to Germany. A treaty between Austria and the Allies had awarded it to Czechoslovakia in 1919. It was home to some three million German-speaking people. Hitler called for its autonomy at first but then demanded its annexation as a means of protecting those people. German troops and tanks massed along the German-Czech border. War appeared imminent.

Diplomats from Britain, France, and Italy met with their German counterparts in an effort to defuel the volatile situation. London and Paris looked toward Washington for help in resolving the growing crisis but none was forthcoming. FDR, hobbled by an isolationist Congress, walked a fine diplomatic line. Hitler blamed the Czech government for the distress of the long-suffering Sudeten Germans. Privately, he wanted an excuse to go to war.

FDR warned of the needless destruction and loss of lives that a war would entail. At the same time, he confirmed American neutrality. In a memo to Hitler, he stated, "The Government of the United States has no political involvement in Europe, and will assume no obligations in the conduct of the present negotiations."[7]

With FDR's "hands-off" affirmation, the fate of the Sudetenland rested largely in the hands of the appeasement-minded Chamberlain. To preserve the peace in

Europe, he agreed to Hitler's demands. In return for the prime minister's concessions, Hitler promised an end to his territorial claims. Chamberlain returned to Britain with a pledge of Anglo-German, claiming before a cheering crowd, "I believe it is peace in our time."[8]

Six months later, Hitler entered Prague and occupied the rest of Czechoslovakia unopposed on March 15, 1939.

Europe Goes to War

Meanwhile, in the United States, the Naval Expansion Act of 1938 authorized a 20 percent across-the-board increase of America's fleet strength. FDR recognized that Hitler must be stopped. In 1939, he asked Congress to repeal the Neutrality Act to permit US arms sales to free European forces. Congress refused. Undeterred, FDR pressed on, dramatically increasing the defense budget and converting

Birth of the Axis

On May 22, Germany and Italy reached a formal agreement called the Rome-Berlin Axis, also known as the Pact of Steel. The name derived from a statement made by Mussolini: "The Berlin-Rome line is not a diaphragm but an axis."[9] The "Axis" was born. It would later extend via the Tripartite Pact into the Berlin-Rome-Tokyo Axis—the Axis powers—on September 27, 1940. The pact called for mutual assistance should any one of the three parties be attacked by a nation not already at war.

America to a military economy. Publicly, he promised America would not fight unless attacked. Privately, he prepared for war.

On August 2, FDR received a letter from Albert Einstein. The German physicist warned him of the potential for developing a bomb with huge explosive force by setting up a nuclear chain reaction in a large mass of uranium. Einstein further cautioned that Germany was already exploring that possibility. FDR quickly authorized a preliminary exploratory program.

FDR's aggressive actions came not a moment too soon.

In Moscow, on August 23, 1939, German and Soviet delegates signed the Soviet-German Nonaggression Pact. Nine days later, Germany invaded Poland on September 1, 1939. And Europe went to war.

AMERICA'S
UNDECLARED WAR

Poland quickly succumbed to Hitler's *Blitzkrieg* (lightning war) on September 27, 1939. Beginning in April 1940, after a brief period of inactivity known as the Phony War, German forces rolled over Denmark, began their conquest of Norway, and swept through the Netherlands and Belgium. France fell to the Germans on June 14, 1940. After the fall of France, Britain stood alone.

Hitler turned his eyes to Britain. Through the extraordinary efforts of Royal Air Force (RAF) pilots—"the Few"—the British repelled Hitler's prelude to invasion over the summer and fall of 1940 in the Battle of Britain.

Newly elected Prime Minister Winston Churchill, while addressing the House of Commons in August 1940, offered memorable praise of the RAF in one sentence: "Never in the field of human conflict was so much owed by so many to so few."[1]

GERMANS INVADE AND BOMB POLAND BRITAIN MOBILISES

Warsaw, Cracow, Nine Other Towns Bombed: Danzig is "Annexed"

FRANCE DECLARES "STATE OF SIEGE"

GERMANY INVADED POLAND TO-DAY. COMPLETE MOBILISATION HAS BEEN ORDERED IN BRITAIN.

Orders in Council for the complete mobilisation of the Navy, Army and Air Force were signed by the King at a Privy Council today. The King also approved other Orders in Council dealing with the emergency.

Warsaw has been bombed. Other German aircraft raided Kursk, Gdynia, Thorn, Bialystock, Grodno, Dihivó and Bydgoszoz. A few hours later, Cracow, Katowice and Czentowice were bombed.

THE EVENING STANDARD LEARNS THAT THE POLISH AMBASSADOR SAW LORD HALIFAX TO-DAY. HE INFORMED THE FOREIGN SECRETARY OF THE GERMAN ATTACK UPON POLAND, WHICH HE SAID CONSTITUTED A CASE OF DIRECT AGGRESSION, AND HE INVOKED THE ANGLO-POLISH TREATY.

French aid has also been invoked.

The French Cabinet met for an hour and 35 minutes. They decided to call Parliament immediately, to order general mobilisation of Army, Navy and Air Force beginning to-morrow, and to proclaim a "state of siege."

The Germans attacked without having delivered any ultimatum.

Attack On Both Sides

They are striking at the "Corridor" both from the East and the West—from the East at the town of Dzialdowa, on the East Prussian frontier, and from the West at Chojnice, about 60 miles from Danzig.

Dzialdowa is about 90 miles north-west of Warsaw.

(Continued on PAGE FOUR)

Air Raid Warning System In Force

LOCAL authorities have been instructed to put their air raid warning systems into full operation.

From now on the sounding of factory sirens and hooters is prohibited, except for giving air raid warnings.

'BRITAIN WILL FULFIL HER OBLIGATIONS'

Parliament Meeting To-night

THE BRITISH CABINET MET TO-DAY. THEY BROKE UP AFTER ONE HOUR AND FIFTY MINUTES.

BOTH HOUSES OF PARLIAMENT ARE MEETING AT SIX O'CLOCK TO-NIGHT. THE PRIME MINISTER IS MAKING A FULL STATEMENT IN THE COMMONS AND AFTERWARDS THE HOUSE IS BEING ASKED TO PASS EMERGENCY LEGISLATION AT ONCE AND TO VOTE CREDITS. LORD HALIFAX IS MAKING A STATEMENT IN THE LORDS.

MEMBERS OF PARLIAMENT WILL BE IN POSSESSION OF THE CORRESPONDENCE BETWEEN GREAT BRITAIN AND GERMANY WHICH WILL BE PUBLISHED IN A WHITE PAPER.

It was pointed out in official circles in London today that if the proclamation to the German people by Herr Hitler should mean, as it would seem to mean, that Germany has declared war on Poland, it can be stated on the highest authority that Great Britain and France are infallibly determined to fulfil to the utmost

(Continued on BACK PAGE)

Front-page headlines of London's *Evening Standard* newspaper announce Germany's invasion of Poland on September 1, 1939, which sparked the start of World War II.

Staffing Up

In early 1940, FDR continued to ready his nation for what he saw as the inevitability of war. He staffed his cabinet with hawks, or those in favor of war, like Henry Stimson (secretary of war) and Frank Knox (secretary of the Navy). And he appointed Harry Hopkins as his emissary and closest personal adviser. Stimson, at seventy-two, was a sharp-witted and vastly experienced wartime administrator, with a keen worldview. Frank Knox, a staunch Republican and former newspaper publisher, helped diversify the political face of FDR's cabinet and facilitate its recruitment. Harry Hopkins had served FDR when he had been governor of New York and had followed him to Washington. No one stood closer to FDR than Harry Hopkins.

At that time, FDR secretly began a long-term correspondence with Churchill, while Churchill was still lord of the admiralty. Their relationship developed into a close working friendship. They worked together toward encouraging neutral America to take a more active anti-Axis role.

Policy and Politics

In the summer of 1940, Gallup polls indicated that 73 percent of Americans favored sending material aid to Britain, but 61 percent felt that staying out of the war still represented America's highest priority. At the same time, legislators—perhaps spurred by the collapse of France in June—began looking seriously at the state of America's military preparedness and a system of selective training.

On September 27, 1940, Germany, Italy, and Japan signed the Tripartite Pact. The pact was meant to ensure

Selective Service

On September 16, 1940, Congress passed the Burke-Wadsworth Act, establishing the first peace-time draft in US history. Selective Service was born. More than sixteen million men between the ages of twenty-one and thirty-five registered for a lottery-style call-up. Some sixteen thousand reported for training in October, in a draft that was projected to expand the peacetime army of about 190,000 men to more than 1.4 million by mid-1941.

Eighty-eight young Selective Service inductees raise their right hands in front of the Los Angeles City Hall and are sworn in to the army on November 19, 1940.

American neutrality. Instead, it promoted increased militant sentiments in the United States. Administration hawks—Stimson, Knox, Secretary of the Treasury Henry Morgenthau Jr. and Secretary of the Interior Harold Ickes—urged FDR to cut off oil exports to Japan to punish its aggressions. Japan imported 80 percent of its oil from the United States.

Secretary of State Cordell Hull, a soft-spoken southerner, favored continued negotiations. Chief of Naval Operations Admiral Harold Stark concurred with Hull. He pointed out that a US oil embargo against Japan would force the island nation to seek other sources of oil. That would pose a threat to Malaya, Burma, the Dutch East Indies, and even the Philippines. Moreover, any military confrontation with Japan in the Pacific would undercut US efforts to aid Britain in the Atlantic. Army Chief of Staff George C. Marshall, recognizing America's unpreparedness for war, noted that the time right then was "as unfavorable a moment as you could choose for provoking trouble."[2]

In October 1940, while battling for a third term as president, FDR heeded the advice of his military advisers and reaffirmed his previous assurances to Americans: "I have said this before, but I shall say it again and again and again: Your boys are not going to be sent into any foreign wars."[3] He won reelection over Republican contender Wendell Willkie by a landslide.

Lend-Lease

In July 1940, Britain sustained the loss of ten destroyers to the German navy over an eleven-day span. Churchill reached out to FDR for help. Skirting the Neutrality Act,

FDR orchestrated a swap of fifty aging US destroyers in return for ninety-nine-year leases on British bases in the Caribbean and Newfoundland.

By year's end, Britain's need for aid was becoming desperate. Churchill called out again for US help. "Give us the tools and we'll finish the job,"[4] he vowed. But Britain was fast running out of money to pay for them.

In a "Fireside Chat" on national radio on December 29, FDR declared that the United States "must be the great arsenal of democracy."[5] How he could justify continued aid to Britain without payment remained an open question. While the president spoke, London was aflame under the heaviest German fire-bombing attack thus far in the war.

In early January 1941, FDR sent Harry Hopkins to London to assess what kind of help Britain needed. At the same time, he proposed a new military-aid bill to Congress. After heated debate, Congress passed "An Act to Promote the Defense of the United States," more popularly known as the Lend-Lease Act, in March. It allowed the United States to supply war material to Britain and other Allied nations—later including the Soviet Union—without requiring payment up front. It thereby dodged the restrictive tenet of the Neutrality Act of 1939.

Atlantic Affairs

In August 1941, FDR and Churchill met secretly at Placentia Bay, Newfoundland, in what is known as the Argentia—or Atlantic—Conference, the first of nine face-to-face wartime conferences. There they drafted the Atlantic Charter, a document outlining the basic tenets for a just peace in the postwar world. The tenets formed the cornerstone of what

Operation Barbarossa

On June 22, 1941, Hitler's latest move shocked the world. He breached the Soviet-German Nonaggression Pact and launched Operation Barbarossa—a treacherous attack on the Soviet Union (USSR). It was named after Holy Roman Emperor Frederick I (surname Barbarossa). Legend held that Frederick would rise from the dead and restore Germany to power. The Soviets entered the war against Germany. Barbarossa would prove to be one of Hitler's greatest miscalculations. Legends do not always hold true.

German *panzers* (tanks) spearhead an infantry attack on Soviet positions on the Eastern Front in 1941.

would later become the United Nations. It was there that FDR proclaimed the Four Freedoms—freedom of speech, freedom of religion, freedom from want, and freedom from fear. They were later memorialized in four paintings by the revered American artist Norman Rockwell.

While the conference succeeded in drafting these important aims, both leaders came away from the meeting somewhat disappointed. Churchill had hoped to persuade FDR to enter the war or to at least substantially increase America's war aid to Britain. Roosevelt hoped the charter would move American public opinion closer to backing a US intervention in the war. Neither man got all he had hoped for, but a lot of something was better than nothing.

In the meantime, FDR's announcement of Lend-Lease aid to Britain had prompted Hitler to shift his western strategy from strategic bombing to attacks on British shipping. In March 1941, he extended the German naval combat zone westward to about Greenland. German U-boats (*Unterseebooten*) began sinking British merchant ships at an alarming rate. Britain lost 650,000 tons of shipping in April alone. FDR knew that Americans would not long tolerate sending billions in war aid to Britain when much of it ended up on the sea bottom.

FDR extended the US coastal security zone eastward so that it overlapped the German western zone by about a third. American ships patrolling this area could provide the RAF and Royal Navy with helpful reconnaissance but could not engage the U-boats. Inevitably, US warships in the region would eventually lead to confrontation.

On September 4, 1941, a U-boat mistook the US destroyer *Greer* for a British destroyer and fired two torpedoes at her. The *Greer* evaded the torpedoes and answered with the release of ten depth charges—the first American shots fired in World War II. Six weeks later, another U-boat torpedoed the US destroyer *Kearny* on October 17. The hit failed to sink her, but it killed eleven crewmembers to claim the first American casualties of the war.

Two weeks later, a third U-boat torpedoed yet another US destroyer, the *Reuben James*. The torpedo struck her amidship, touching off her munitions magazine, splitting her apart, and sending her to the bottom. One hundred and fifteen American sailors died. FDR fumed at the report and delared, "The shooting has started. And history has recorded who fired the first shot."[6] FDR commenced an "undeclared war" against German U-boats in the Atlantic. By then, US neutrality existed in name only.

Neutral No Longer

Meanwhile, Japan had moved large forces into French Indochina (now Vietnam). FDR countered by stiffening US

On October 1, 1941, a German U-boat torpedoed the US destroyer *Reuben James* and sent her to the bottom of the ocean with 115 American sailors.

policy toward Japan. In July 1941, he froze Japanese assets and cut off oil shipments to Japan. In Tokyo, Japanese naval leaders began planning to attack Pearl Harbor, the Philippines, and other Pacific bases, to open the sea route to the oil-rich Dutch East Indies. At the same time, Japanese envoys continued to talk peace at negotiations in Washington, DC.

Secret Japanese code intercepts—code-named "Magic"—broken by the United States in September 1940 revealed the imminence of a Japanese attack. The timing and location of the attack remained unclear.

In the autumn of 1941, FDR authorized a crash program of atomic development recommended by a committee of the National Academy of Sciences. On December 6, a group of physicists met secretly with FDR. They knew that the Germans and Japanese were already working on research aimed at creating atom bombs. Physicist Arthur Compton warned, "We must get them first."[7] FDR directed the group to determine the feasibility of an atomic weapon within six months.

The next day, Japanese warplanes attacked Pearl Harbor. America could remain neutral no longer.

AMERICA JOINS
THE FIGHT

Japanese air strikes devastated the US Pacific Fleet at Pearl Harbor on December 7, 1941. A joint congressional committee called the attack the "greatest military and naval disaster in our Nation's history."[1] *"Remember Pearl Harbor!"* became America's battle cry. America joined the fight against the Axis powers, but many months would elapse before it could strike back offensively.

In the immediate aftermath of the Pearl Harbor attack, Japanese forces seized Guam and Wake Island, threatened the Philippines, toppled Hong Kong, and advanced deep into Malaya (now Malaysia). Meanwhile, the German war machine bogged down in the fierce Russian winter within sight of the Kremlin.

Europe First

Faced with a two-front war and his first major decision, FDR met with Churchill and the two opted to focus first on defeating Germany. Meanwhile, the US Pacific Fleet would

This is one of many patriotic posters rallying Americans to "Remember Pearl Harbor" and urging them to adopt a wartime posture in work, in service, and in sacrifice.

strive as best it could to contain Japanese expansion. The decision became known as the "Europe First" strategy. It met with initial resistance at home because most Americans wanted to seek immediate revenge against the Japanese. FDR held fast to the European commitment, and the Allies focused first on defeating Hitler.

From December 22, 1941, to January 14, 1942, FDR, Churchill, and their advisers held a conference called Arcadia in Washington, DC, to synchronize military efforts. They hammered out future strategies and devices for use in a coordinated war effort. First off, they established the Combined Chiefs of Staff (CCS) by merging the US Joint Chiefs of Staff (JCS) with the British Chiefs of Staff (COS).

Topics of discussion included a North Africa invasion, action against the Japanese in the Philippines, and Lend-Lease for the USSR. FDR released a customary recap of the meeting he called the Declaration of the United Nations. It committed the Allies to making no separate peace with the enemy and using their full resources until victory was achieved. Reporting on American readiness, senior British representative Field Marshal John G. Dill noted, "This country is the most highly organized for peace you can imagine ... Never have I seen a country so utterly unprepared for War and so soft."[2]

The First Six Months

Meanwhile, the Japanese war machine continued to roll in Asia, securing Malaya and Singapore, seizing Burma and Thailand in the China-Burma-India (CBI) theater, and

Japanese Internment

Shortly after the attack on Pearl Harbor, a wave of anti-Japanese hysteria swept the nation. Americans feared additional attacks or sabotage by the Japanese, particularly on the West Coast. On January 14, 1942, FDR issued Presidential Proclamation 2537 that enabled the arrest and detention of enemy aliens that violated restricteccccd areas such as ports and military areas.

A month later, on February 19, FDR reluctantly issued Executive Order 9066 to the War Department to calm the fears of many Americans. It called for the internment of some 120,000 Japanese living mostly on the West Coast— seventy-seven thousand American citizens and forty-three thousand legal and illegal residents.

Long after the end of World War II, Congress enacted the Civil Liberties Act of 1988 to compensate every surviving Japanese-American internee with an apology and a check for $20,000.

After the Japanese attack on Pearl Harbor, US soldiers supervise the relocation of a group of Japanese Americans from their homes on the American west coast to one of ten specially built internment camps.

extending its reach to the Philippines and the Dutch East Indies.

In the Philippines, General Douglas MacArthur, on FDR's orders, shifted his command to General Jonathan M. Wainwright and left for Australia on March 12. MacArthur vowed to return. US forces on Bataan surrendered on April 9. Wainwright retreated to Corregidor Island—"the Rock"—with a small group of holdouts.

When urged by a war correspondent to flee the island, Wainwright replied, "I have been one of the 'battling

Japanese victors in the Battle of Corregidor march off the fallen American defenders of the rocky fortress in Manila Bay.

bastards of Bataan' and I'll play the same role on the Rock as long as it is humanly possible."[3] The men on Corregidor surrendered to the Japanese on May 6.

On March 11, physicists informed FDR that an atomic bomb was indeed theoretically feasible. "I think the whole thing should be pushed not only in regard to development but also with due regard for time," FDR replied. "This is very much of the essence."[4] FDR prioritized its development and assigned the task—soon to be known as the Manhattan Project—to Secretary Henry Stimson and the War Department. Stimson named army engineer General Leslie R. Groves to direct the program. Groves in turn appointed physicist J. Robert Oppenheimer to head the group that would design and build the bomb.

Across the Atlantic, the Germans encircled Stalingrad in Russia and defeated the British in Libya at Tobruk in June 1942. America's first major victory in the Pacific came that same month at Battle of Midway. In a four-day battle that marked the turning point in the Pacific, dive bombers from the US carriers *Enterprise* and *Yorktown* sank four Japanese carriers and a heavy cruiser. Japan's losses included 275 aircraft and roughly 4,800 personnel, many of them irreplaceable pilots. The United States lost 307 men, 150 planes, the carrier *Yorktown*, and the destroyer *Hammann*.

In an after-battle communique, Pacific Fleet commander Admiral Chester W. Nimitz proudly declared: "Pearl Harbor has now been partially avenged. Vengeance will not be complete until Japanese sea power is reduced to impotence ... Perhaps we will be forgiven if we claim that

A flight of Douglas SBD Dauntless dive bombers fly over their carrier in a tight wedge formation. Dauntless bombers such as these decimated the Japanese fleet at the Battle of Midway.

we are about midway to our objective."[5] After six months on the defensive, America was striking back.

America Battles Back

In the summer of 1942, FDR and Navy chief Admiral Ernest J. King consulted over charts in the Map Room and started putting together an offensive plan for the Pacific theater. On August 7, US Marines landed on Guadalcanal Island in the South Pacific to launch the first American land offensive of the war. Fierce land and sea action raged on the island and offshore for the next six months. American land, sea, and air forces finally succeeded in driving the Japanese off the island in February 1943.

FDR cabled Stalin news of the American victory: "We have hit the Japanese very hard in the Solomon Islands. We have probably broken the backbone of the power of their Fleet. They have still too many carriers to suit me, but soon we may well sink some more of them."[6]

The Soviets were now bearing the brunt of German advances. Stalin started pressuring Britain and the United States for a second front in the western sector of the war in Europe to relieve his own beleaguered forces. US leaders such as Secretary Stimson, Generals George C. Marshall and Dwight D. ("Ike") Eisenhower, and Admiral King wanted to strike directly at Europe. Churchill felt Allied forces were not yet ready for a cross-channel invasion. He wanted to strike at the "soft underbelly"[7] of occupied Europe.

FDR effected a compromise in Operation Torch. It called for a landing in North Africa, followed by the occupation of Algeria and Morocco, then controlled by Vichy France. FDR selected General Eisenhower to head the Allied forces. The combined US-British operation began on November 8, 1942.

Anglo-American forces executed three successful amphibious landings: one near Casablanca in Morocco, led by General George S. Patton, and two in Algeria at Oran and Algiers. All three sites were then controlled by Vichy French forces. After overcoming light resistance from the French, the Allied forces advanced eastward. Four days earlier, the British Eighth Army under Field Marshal

Bernard L. Montgomery had stopped Field Marshal Erwin J. E. Rommel's Afrika Korps at El Alamein and was advancing westward. Hitler recalled Rommel in March. The western and eastern Allied forces contained the Germans in Tunisia in April. Some 275,000 German and Italian troops surrendered in May 1943. Operation Torch ended.

Europe's Soft Underbelly

In January 1943, after the success of the North Africa invasion, FDR flew to meet with Churchill in Casablanca, Morocco, to discuss future war aims. (Stalin was invited but did not attend the meeting.) During the transatlantic flight, FDR turned ghastly pale during air turbulence at fifteen thousand feet (4.6 km). His personal physician, Admiral Ross T. McIntire, worried "about the President's bad heart."[8] His concern marked an early acknowledgment of FDR's coronary condition.

At Casablanca, FDR proclaimed that the war must end with the "unconditional surrender" of all Axis forces. The two leaders discussed plans for an Italian Campaign and again put off the cross-channel invasion.

FDR and Churchill met again in Washington, DC, in May (Third Washington Conference; codenamed Trident Conference) and decided to invade Sicily that summer. They postponed the cross-channel invasion until May 1944, while agreeing to step up air attacks against Germany and increase war efforts in the Pacific.

The invasion of Sicily—code-named Operation Husky—launched on July 10, 1943. General Patton's US Seventh Army and General Montgomery's British Eighth

Soviet Successes

After a six-month siege at Stalingrad, the Soviets forced the surrender of the German Sixth Army and its allies on February 2, 1943. Of the original 300,000 Germans, only ninety thousand remained. Their surrender capped a huge victory for the Soviets.

Five months later, in the Battle of Kursk (July 3–13, 1943), the Soviets inflicted heavy losses on the Germans. The battle involved six thousand tanks and four thousand aircraft. German losses included seventy thousand killed and 2,900 tanks and some 1,400 aircraft destroyed. Soviet casualties totaled about 160,000, but the victory effectively won the war for the Soviets.

Soviet tanks and troops held fast against the German attackers in the snow and ice and eventually claimed victory at Stalingrad.

Quadrant

In August, FDR and Churchill met in Quebec (First Quebec Conference; codenamed Quadrant Conference). They approved an outline for the Normandy landing and discussed a second landing in the south of France. A further discussion centered on cooperating in the development and production of the atomic bomb. They agreed never to use the bomb against each other or against a third party without their mutual consent. Further, they agreed "to bring the Tube Alloys project to fruition at the earliest moment."[9] "Tube Alloys" was code for the atomic effort.

Army attacked German and Italian defenders in the west and east, respectively. Allied forces quickly crushed all Axis resistance and converged at the key port of Messina on August 17. But 100,000 Axis troops escaped to mainland Italy to fight another day.

On September 3, the Allies crossed the Strait of Messina and invaded southern Italy. Italy surrendered five days later on September 8. In a joint declaration, FDR and Churchill encouraged the people of Italy from afar: "Now is the time for every Italian to strike his blow … Strike hard and strike home. Have faith in your future. All will come well."[10] The long and bloody march up the Italian boot began.

A WORLD AT WAR

From November 23 to 26, 1943, FDR and Churchill met again at the Cairo Conference (code-named Sextant) in Egypt. This time, they met for the first time with Generalissimo Chiang Kai-shek, Nationalist China's president and war leader. Stalin declined to attend. The three leaders agreed on future operations against Japan and the postwar return of Chinese territories seized by Japan, such as Manchukuo and Formosa.

FDR, looking ahead to China's future role in the Pacific, noted, "I really feel that it is a triumph to have got the [then] four hundred and twenty-five million Chinese in on the Allied side. This will be very useful 25 or 50 years hence, even though China cannot contribute much military or naval support for the moment."[1]

Tehran Conference

FDR and Churchill traveled from Cairo to Tehran, Iran, to meet with Soviet leader Joseph Stalin for the first time. The conference (code-named Eureka) between the Big Three—

Seated together on the lawn at the historic Cairo Conference in November 1943, Generalissimo Chiang Kai-shek grins for the camera while President Franklin D. Roosevelt smiles at a pensive-looking Prime Minister Winston Churchill.

as the three leaders were called—took place from November 28 to December 1, 1943. Stalin renewed his insistence on a second front in France. FDR and Churchill announced their decision to launch an invasion at Normandy (Operation Overlord) in May 1944. Stalin agreed to their Normandy decision. The three leaders further approved the postwar demilitarizing of Germany and the establishment of occupation zones.

FDR used his charm in an effort to cement a crucial new friendship with Stalin. His overtures to the Soviet leader came to the detriment of his relationship with Churchill. Their rapport had already begun to show signs of strain. Churchill held an innate distrust of Stalin and made no secret of it. Moreover, Churchill hoped for a continuation of British imperialism in the postwar world; FDR, in the manner of his democratic predecessor Woodrow Wilson, envisioned an end to colonialism in the new world order. The two worldviews mixed like oil and water.

At a dinner hosted by Stalin, FDR suddenly became violently ill and was escorted to his room. His physician diagnosed the problem as indigestion. Roosevelt recovered by the next morning. Most of those present blamed the borscht (Russian beet soup) and soon forgot the incident. Despite Churchill's displeasure at FDR's attempts to curry Stalin's favor, the three leaders ended their meeting on a cordial note. "We leave here friends in fact, in spirit, and in purpose,"[2] they said collectively.

FDR stopped at Tunis on his return trip from Tehran to meet with Eisenhower. "Well, Ike," the president said, "you are going to command Overlord."[3] To Ike fell the task of planning and executing the largest amphibious operation in military history.

Island Assaults

Meanwhile, in the Pacific theater, American troops landed on Bougainville in the Solomon Islands on November 1. Three weeks later, in the Central Pacific, US forces assaulted two atolls in the Gilbert Islands, Makin and Tarawa (Operation Galvanic) on November 20. The Army's Twenty-Seventh Infantry Division quickly subdued a small Japanese garrison on Makin. Troops of the Second Marine Division found much tougher going on Betio, Tarawa's main islet. Japanese commander Admiral Maichi Shibasaki had boasted that the tiny islet—three miles (4.8 km) long by half a mile (.8 km) wide—could "withstand assault by a million men for a hundred years."[4]

After two days of fierce fighting, Colonel David M. Shoup, Medal of Honor winner and future Marine commandant, signaled, "We are winning."[5] Tarawa fell to the Marines on the fourth day but at a great cost.

Unlike the European war strategy built on international cooperation, the Allies left the war against Japan almost exclusively in the hands of the Americans. The US Joint Chiefs divided the Pacific theater into two areas of operation: the Pacific Ocean Area, headed by Admiral Chester W. Nimitz, and the Southwest Pacific Area, commanded by General Douglas MacArthur. Both leaders reported directly to the Joint Chiefs.

A two-prong strategy evolved from the two commands, as American forces embarked on two island-hopping paths to Japan's home islands. Nimitz's route led westward across the Central Pacific and through the Gilberts, Marshalls, Marianas, Carolines, and Palaus toward the Philippines or Formosa (now Taiwan). MacArthur's path advanced northward from New Guinea to the Philippines. The strategy called for the two prongs to converge at the Philippines, after either neutralizing or bypassing Japanese strongholds along the way.

MacArthur, having pledged to return to the Philippines, and fearing naval strategists would convince FDR to bypass them, complained vigorously to FDR. A harried Roosevelt reassured the general to the contrary. "The Philippines will

Costly Mistakes at Bloody Betio

The Gilbert Islands lie about 2,500 miles (4,023 km) southwest of Hawaii. Tarawa forms a part of the island group. Admiral Nimitz chose it as a starting point in his "island-hopping" campaign in the Central Pacific. Admiral Harry W. Hill, commander of the invasion fleet, promised to pound the islet Betio with naval gunfire and dive bombers "until hell wouldn't have it."[6] The Americans expected few of the coral reef's 4,700 Japanese defenders to survive the pounding. They were mistaken. The Japanese were so deeply entrenched on Betio in bunkers and pillboxes that most of them survived.

American planners estimated the reef would be covered by five feet (1.5 m) of water at the time of the landing. They were mistaken. Their estimates were based on a flood tide season when tides are at their highest. The assault forces actually went in during a neap tide season. Tides were at their lowest. Because of the miscalculation, Marine landing craft and amphibious tractors ran aground on the reef in three feet (.9 m) of water. Marines were forced out of their assault boats into waist-deep water far from shore. Many were cut down by withering Japanese gunfire from the beach. Those who reached shore engaged in seventy-five-plus hours of "the bitterest fighting in the history of the Marine Corps."[7]

The Marines suffered nearly three thousand casualties, including 984 dead. Only seventeen of the Japanese defenders survived. Mistakes were, and are, costly.

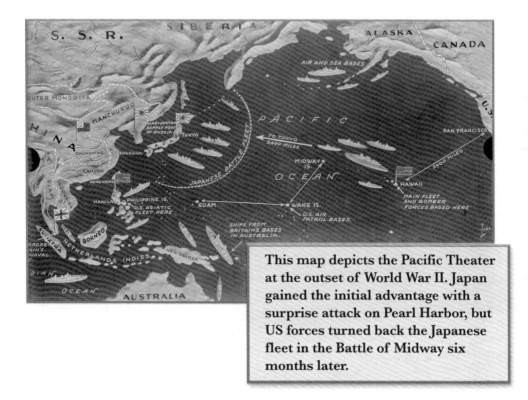

This map depicts the Pacific Theater at the outset of World War II. Japan gained the initial advantage with a surprise attack on Pearl Harbor, but US forces turned back the Japanese fleet in the Battle of Midway six months later.

not be bypassed," he said. FDR then requested two aspirins from his physician, saying, "In all my life, nobody has ever talked to me the way MacArthur did."[8]

MacArthur landed Allied forces near Hollandia in Dutch New Guinea on April 22, 1944. The US Army's Forty-First Division stormed ashore without resistance. The Japanese staff headquartered in the former Dutch administrative capital were completely surprised. Most of the eleven thousand personnel stationed there fled into the hills. Twenty-two miles (35 kilometers) to the west, the US Twenty-Fourth Division landed at Tanahmerah Bay. At the same time, a regiment of the Forty-First Division secured Aitape, some 120 miles (193 km) to the east, to complete a

Merrill's Marauders: Mission Accomplished

Beginning in February 1944, US General Frank D. Merrill led the first major Allied counteroffensive in the China-Burma-India theater. His 5307th Composite Unit—better known as "Merrill's Marauders"—set out on a series of guerrilla operations in Burma (now Myanmar). Their mission: oust the Japanese from the Burmese city of Myitkyina and secure supply routes to China. Merrill and his Marauders, supplied by airdrops, battled near-impenetrable jungles, leeches, twenty-foot (6-meters) pythons, unbearable heat, and hunger, but they accomplished their mission.

General Frank Merrill (with map), leader of the famous Merrill's Marauders, and his staff plot their next move against Japanese forces somewhere in Burma (now Myanmar).

three-pronged attack. The successful landings were aided immensely by General George C. Kenney's Fifth Air Force. His command had virtually destroyed all but a handful of Japanese aircraft on the New Guinea coast.

"The operation throws a loop of envelopment around the [Japanese] Eighteenth Army dispersed along the coast of New Guinea,"[9] MacArthur reported triumphantly. He had taken his first step on his return to the Philippines.

Italian Campaign

Meanwhile, on the other side of the world, US and British forces drove up the Italian boot. Advancing swiftly, General Mark W. Clark's US Fifth Army liberated Naples on October 1, 1943. Neapolitans cheered the conquerors. By late 1943, however, the Allied advance bogged down at the Gustav Line, a heavily fortified German defense line that spanned the Italian Peninsula about 115 miles (185 km) south of Rome. A reinforced German army of twenty-three divisions—215,000 troops on line and 265,000 in reserve—held the Allied armies in check for several months.

The Allies failed in three attempts to break the line. German and Allied forces engaged in some of the fiercest fighting of the war there. They fought in some of the harshest terrain and under some of the most extreme weather conditions—rain, mud, snow, ice, and freezing temperatures—endured by fighting men anywhere else in the European theater. In an attempt to draw some of the German defenders off the Gustav Line, the Allies launched an amphibious operation at Anzio.

On May 23, the Allied VI Corps finally broke out of the Anzio beachhead. It linked up with II Corps of the US

"A Stranded Whale"

With the Germans and Allies stalemated along the Gustav Line, General Sir Harold Alexander, commander in chief of the Allied ground forces, called for an amphibious end run. He hoped to divert some of the German forces and weaken their defenses. His plan, called Operation Shingle, produced less than desirable results. Alexander appointed US General John P. Lucas to lead an expeditionary force in an assault on Anzio, about thirty-five miles (56 km) south of Rome on the west coast of Italy.

The operation commenced on January 22, 1944. Lucas's VI Corps—British First Infantry Division and US Third Infantry Division—landed on the beach at Anzio. German Field Marshal Albert Kesselring, commander of all German forces in Italy, rushed General Eberhard von Mackensen's Fourteenth Army to establish a firm perimeter about the Allied corps on February 3. The Allies dug in at their beachhead, which was by then fifteen miles (24 km) long and seven miles (11 km) deep. They twice repulsed German counterattacks but remained trapped in place for more than four months.

The intended Allied flanking maneuver turned into an agonizing battle of attrition. Allied casualties totaled seven thousand killed and thirty-six thousand wounded. German losses numbered an estimated total of eleven thousand. Of the Anzio operation, Winston Churchill later said, "I had hoped we were hurling a wildcat onto the shore, but all we got was a stranded whale."[10]

Fifth Army, which had breached the Gustav Line and was moving north. The Fifth Army entered Rome on June 4. The next day, FDR, in his only Fireside Chat of the year thus far, told the American people, "The first of the Axis capitals is now in our hands. One up and two to go!"[11] The thrill of victory would soon subside, however. Gigantic Allied forces, assembled in Great Britain over many months, were girding for the largest landing of them all.

TURNING THE TIDE

O ver the past many months, the Allies—mainly the United States and Britain—had been gathering millions of men, thousands of ships and tanks, and tens of thousands of vehicles in Britain. History's greatest armada was formed under the leadership of General Dwight D. ("Ike") Eisenhower, supreme commander of the Allied Expeditionary Force, or SCAEF. Ike described the invasion force as "a great human spring, coiled for the moment when its energy should be released and it would vault the English Channel in the greatest amphibious assault ever assembled."[1] The spring was released on June 6, 1944—D-Day.

Operation Overlord

Britain had begun planning for a return to France since the evacuation of its forces at Dunkirk in the spring of 1940. Two months before D-Day, the projected invasion date, some twelve thousand Allied aircraft began destroying railways in France and Belgium to impede the enemy's ability

British troops from the Lancashire and Middlesex regiments wade ashore at Sword Beach in Normandy, France, on June 6, 1944—D-Day.

to rush troops to the battlefront. As D-Day drew closer, they targeted bridges in northwestern France. On D-minus-2, they blasted airfields within a 130-mile (209-kilometer) radius of the landing beaches. Then the time to execute the plan arrived.

A gale delayed the invasion at Normandy on June 4, 1944. Two days later, a thirty-six-hour window of clear weather presented itself. General Eisenhower signaled the go-ahead. Shortly after dark on June 5, the invasion armada headed for a forty-mile (64-km) stretch of coastline in France between the Orne River and the Cotentin peninsula. It consisted of some 4,400 ships and landing craft, transporting 176,475 troops, 20,111 vehicles, and 1,500 tanks, under an umbrella of twelve thousand aircraft.

Before retiring that night, Winston Churchill commented gravely to his wife Clementine. "Do you realize," he asked, "that by the time you wake up in the morning twenty thousand men may have been killed?"[2]

Facing the invaders stood Hitler's vaunted Atlantic Wall: a chain of fortifications containing concrete bunkers, pillboxes, tank traps, mines, beach obstacles, and more. It ran along Europe's coastline from Norway to the Spanish border. Eisenhower's counterpart, Field Marshal Gerd von Rundstedt, held overall command of the German defense forces, about fifty infantry and ten Panzer (tank) divisions. Responding to Allied deceptions and diversions, he had expected the Allies to land at Calais. The French port represented the shortest route across the channel. Accordingly, Rundstedt concentrated the bulk of his forces in that area.

The daring Field Marshal Erwin Rommel, who had gained repute as the "Desert Fox" in North Africa, was charged with defending the Normandy region. He commanded Army Group B. His defensive strategy differed from that of Rundstedt, his superior. Rundstedt favored allowing the enemy to land and striking them inland before they could consolidate their forces. Rommel wanted to engage the enemy on the beaches. "The war will be won or lost on the beaches," he told his aide. "[T]he first 24 hours will be decisive ... for the Allies, as well as Germany, it will be the longest day."[3]

Marshal Erwin Rommel (*left*) discusses German strategy with Marshal Gerd von Rundstedt in January 1944.

In the end, the two marshals compromised, positioning the infantry forward and the tanks back. This resulted in little coordination between them.

Operation Overlord launched at 0200 on June 6. One British and two US airborne divisions—the Eighty-Second and 101st—dropped behind the beaches to secure exit routes for the seaborne forces. After a preliminary naval and air bombardment of the landing zones by battleships, cruisers, destroyers, and aircraft, the first waves of infantry and tanks hit the beaches at 0630, just after sunrise.

"The Longest Day"

Field Marshal Bernard Montgomery, of British Eighth Army fame, served as field commander of all Allied ground forces. General Omar N. Bradley's US First Army (V and VII Corps) stormed ashore at beaches designated Omaha and Utah. The British Second Army (I and III Corps), under General Miles C. Dempsey, landed to the left of the Americans at beaches named Gold, Juno, and Sword.

The assaults went well on the British beaches. One Canadian and two British divisions met little resistance and pressed inland toward Caen for about seven miles (11 km). At Utah, VII Corps sustained light casualties and drove inland to quickly hook up with elements of the Eighty-Second Airborne Division. At Omaha, the situation quickly turned grim. The Germans had moved in an elite division. Withering machine-gun fire from emplacements along the coastal cliffs inflicted more than two thousand casualties on exposed V Corps troops on the beach below. Nevertheless, V Corps held on and weathered the storm of German resistance. By the end of Rommel's "longest day," the Allies had landed some 150,000 troops and the equipment and supplies to sustain them. The British, with a huge assist from the Americans, had returned to France.

On D-Day evening, FDR led the nation in prayer, praying first for American sons in harm's way: "Lead them straight and true; give strength to their arms, stoutness to their hearts, steadfastness in their faith."[4]

The German High Command still thought the Normandy landings were a feint. They held their main forces in the Calais area. And they failed until too late to commit their armored reserve at Normandy. By June 12, the Allies had landed 300,000 troops and fifty thousand vehicles ashore in Normandy. Cherbourg fell to the Allies on June 27, to set the stage for the breakout at St.-Lô in July.

In the east, the Soviets launched Operation Bagration, a campaign aimed at clearing Belorussia and destroying Hitler's Army Group Center. It commenced on June 22, 1944, sixteen days after D-Day and three years from the date of Germany's invasion of the USSR. Bagration would kill some 157,000 German troops and destroy two thousand tanks and fifty-seven thousand vehicles.

Grave Prediction

On July 21, FDR boarded the US heavy cruiser *Baltimore* for a meeting with Admiral Nimitz and General MacArthur in Pearl Harbor during July 27-28. Before embarking, FDR underwent a pre-travel examination by Navy cardiologist Commander Howard Bruenn. The examination revealed that the president was suffering from hardening of the arteries, a failing left ventricle, and soaring high blood pressure. His BP readings registered as high as 218 over 120.

Date to Remember

On July 20, 1944, Democrats in Chicago nominated FDR for a fourth term. Republicans had already nominated New York Governor Thomas E. Dewey as their candidate for president. As FDR's running mate, the Democrats nominated Harry S. Truman, a former haberdasher from Missouri. At that time, it seems unlikely that either FDR or Truman envisioned the enormity of the task that fate held in store for the latter.

That same day in Europe, an assassination attempt on Adolf Hitler failed at his "Wolf's Lair" headquarters in East Prussia. Hitler survived the blast of a bomb misplaced beneath a conference table. By a quirk of fate, hopes for shortening the war vanished in a botched effort to rid the world of one of its evilest entities on a date to remember.

High-ranking Nazi Hermann Göring (*center*) examines the bomb-blast damage at Hitler's Rastenburg headquarters after a failed attempt on Hitler's life on July 20, 1944.

Admiral Chester Nimitz points at the Japanese home islands on a map of the Pacific Theater during a strategy meeting with General Douglas MacArthur, President Franklin D. Roosevelt, and Admiral William Leahy.

At Pearl Harbor, FDR asked, "Douglas, where do we go from here?"[5] MacArthur replied, "Leyte, Mr. President, and then Luzon!"[6] Nimitz preferred Formosa, but FDR sanctioned the liberation of the Philippines. FDR's gaunt appearance shocked those at the meeting. MacArthur, confiding in one of his officers, said, "the mark of death is on him. In six months, he'll be in his grave."[7]

Rolling Back the Enemy

Meanwhile, in the Central Pacific, American Marines and soldiers invaded Saipan in the Marianas on June 15, 1944.

Thirty thousand Japanese defenders fought fanatically. By day's end, some two thousand Marines were dead or wounded, but twenty thousand were on the island. The Army's Twenty-Seventh Infantry Regiment came ashore as reinforcements. Soldiers and Marines fought side by side. On June 20, about three thousand remaining Japanese soldiers emerged from concealed caves and bunkers and counterattacked in a desperate, screaming *banzai* charge. The US forces secured the island two days later. Of the original thirty thousand defenders, only about one thousand remained. American casualties totaled 16,525 dead and wounded.

Marines, supported by army troops, continued their island campaigns, landing on Guam, the largest island of the Marianas, on July 21. Their combined forces annihilated a Japanese garrison of about twelve thousand. The Americans casualties totaled about three thousand.

Back in France, General George S. Patton's tanks spearheaded a breakout from the Normandy beachhead at St.-Lô on August 1, 1944. Two weeks later, on August 15, the US Seventh Army and Free-French units under General Alexander McCarrell Patch landed in southern France in Operation Dragoon. The race for the Rhine began. Patton's Third Army led the drive across France. And the tide of battle in Europe began to turn.

Nearing the End

From September 12 to 16, FDR and Churchill met again in Quebec (Second Quebec Conference; codenamed the Octagon Conference). The two leaders discussed plans for the occupation of Germany and the defeat of Japan.

Sea Battles

The rollback of Japanese forces was greatly aided by resounding US naval victories in the Philippine Sea on June 19, 1944, and in Leyte Gulf during October 23-26, 1944.

In the Philippine Sea, Admiral Soemu Toyoda ordered a fleet of nine carriers and eighteen battleships and cruisers to engage US warships covering the invasion of Saipan. The US Fifth Fleet sent a task force of fifteen carriers to intercept the Japanese fleet. In the ensuing air battle, 450 American planes dueled 430 Japanese aircraft. American pilots called the fray the "Marianas Turkey Shoot." Only 100 Japanese planes survived, against thirty American losses.

At Leyte Gulf, most of the remaining Japanese fleet clashed with elements of the US Third and Seventh Fleets in one of the largest and most complex naval battles of the war. The battle cost the Japanese three battleships, four carriers, ten cruisers, and nine destroyers. The Americans lost three carriers, two destroyers, and a destroyer escort. The decisive US naval victory opened the way for the Allied advance to the Philippines.

MacArthur returned to the Philippines on October 20, 1944. Wading ashore at Leyte, he announced, "I have returned."[8]

The Grumman F6F Hellcat fighter outfought its Japanese adversaries in the Pacific and claimed a great victory in the Battle of the Philippine Sea in June 1944.

Despite flagging health and the unexplained loss of thirty pounds, FDR left Quebec and campaigned for reelection. His efforts were rewarded when he handily won reelection on November 7, to become the only US four-term president.

Four days later, Hitler ordered his generals to prepare for a break through Allied lines in the Ardennes and a subsequent drive on Antwerp. As 1944 drew to a close, a major German counteroffensive loomed large.

TRIUMPH AND TRAGEDY

On December 16, 1944, a snowy night during the coldest winter in Europe in fifty-four years, Hitler's armies launched a last desperate effort in the Ardennes to turn back the Allied tide. The Ardennes is a heavily wooded region in southeast Belgium and northeast France. Hitler hoped to stabilize his western front by cutting through thinly manned US positions there and driving through to Antwerp, Belgium's major port. To this end, he massed twenty-five divisions—eleven of them armored—along a sixty-mile (97-kilometer) front in the Ardennes area, deployed as three armies.

Hitler called his offensive *Unternehmen Wacht am Rhein* ("Operation Watch on the Rhine"). His massive assault caught six US divisions of resting, newly arrived troops by surprise and created a large "bulge" in the Allied lines. Thus, historians would later record the largest land battle fought by American troops in World War II as the Battle of the Bulge (December 16, 1944–January 28, 1945).

German Type II tanks rumble through Ardennes Forest during the Battle of France in 1940. Larger, more powerful *panzers* retraced their route during the Battle of the Bulge in December 1944.

Countless acts of American heroism—many by noncombatants such as clerks, cooks, and others—coupled with rapid troop reinforcements of some 200,000 troops in four days, enabled the US forces to temporarily contain the German penetration.

At the French town of Bastogne, the Forty-Seventh Panzer Corps surrounded elements of the 101st Airborne Division before Christmas. When the German commander called for the Americans to surrender, 101st commander General Anthony McAuliffe replied, "Nuts!"[1] Patton's Third Army relieved the besieged paratroopers on

December 26. General Eisenhower quickly shuffled his ground forces and rushed reinforcements into the bulge area and redeployed Allied air forces that had been grounded by bad weather.

After December 23, heavy Allied fighter-bomber attacks decimated German columns. Elements of the US First and Third Armies pushed back and reduced the bulge in late December and early January. Faced with a fast-vanishing salient, Hitler recalled his armies in late January, and his short-lived offensive ended. His brief incursion cost Germany 100,000 casualties, one thousand aircraft, and mountains of irreplaceable weapons and equipment. American casualties totaled sixty-six thousand. Hitler faced more bad news in the east.

General Georgy Zhukov's forces, leading from the center of the Soviet advance, captured the Polish capital of Warsaw on January 17, 1945. The air distance between Berlin and Warsaw is 322 miles (518 km). Hitler and Germany were running out of both time and space.

Yalta Conference

From February 4 to 11, FDR, Churchill, and Stalin met at Yalta (code-named Argonaut Conference) in Crimea. By then, FDR's health was failing fast. "The signs of deterioration seemed to me unmistakable," W. Averell Harriman, US ambassador to the Soviet Union, remarked later. "Nevertheless, he had blocked out definite objectives which he had clearly in his mind and he carried on the negotiations to this end with his usual skill and perception."[2]

At Yalta, the three leaders solidified final plans for the defeat of Germany and plans for postwar Europe,

The "Big Three" Allied leaders of World War II confer at the Yalta Conference in February 1945. Seated from left to right are British prime minister Winston Churchill, American president Franklin D. Roosevelt, and Soviet premier Joseph Stalin. Admiral Leahy and General Marshall stand behind them in the center at Livadia Palace.

established a date for a United Nations Conference, and set conditions for the USSR's entry in the war against Japan. The latter provision granted railway rights in Manchuria and territorial concessions for the USSR.

They also issued the Declaration on Liberated Europe. It called for all people to have the right to choose their own government by democratic, free elections. The most contentious issue granted the occupying Soviet army the right to establish a temporary government in Poland. Stalin promised to hold free elections, but he instead tightened his grip on eastern Europe. Some critics still fault FDR for conceding too much to Stalin at Yalta, at the loss of eastern European freedom.

On March 1, FDR reported to Congress on Yalta. He told the legislators he had repeated his demands for unconditional surrender. That meant, he said, "the end of the Nazi Party and all of its barbaric laws and institutions."[3] He said the Yalta agreements should end "unilateral action, exclusive alliances, spheres of influence, the balances of power"[4] and many other measures that have failed the world for centuries. They did not.

The War Heats Up

During March 9-10, US B-29 Superfortresses dropped 2,000 tons (1814 metric tons) of incendiary bombs on Tokyo, incinerating the Japanese capital and killing between eighty thousand and 130,000 civilians in history's worst firestorm.

On April 1, 1945—Easter Sunday—two Marine and two Army divisions invaded Okinawa, and the last major battle of the war commenced.

In Western Europe, George Patton's US Fifth Division crossed the Rhine on March 22 and was driving eastward against crumbling German defenses. Soviet forces were advancing rapidly all along the Eastern Front. Stalin told Eisenhower that the capture of Berlin was not important, then ordered his generals to take it before the Western Allies.

Battle for Iwo Jima

US Marines landed on Iwo Jima on February 19, 1945. Iwo Jima is a small island in the Bonin group, 746 miles (1,201 km) south of Tokyo. Admiral Nimitz targeted the island as a forward airfield site to support the impending attack on Japan's home islands.

The island's defenses consisted of a mixed Japanese army and navy garrison of twenty-one thousand men commanded by General Tadamichi Kuribayashi. Under his direction, the defenders had turned the island into a bleak fortress of artillery, mortar, and automatic-gun emplacements, all linked together by miles of trench lines.

The American assault force numbered 250,000 troops, including three divisions of Marines, and more than nine hundred ships. Nine thousand Marines clambered ashore in the first wave. The Japanese held fire until the Marines jammed the beach with men and equipment, then unleashed a barrage of murderous fire from high above on Mount Suribachi on the island's southern tip. Marine casualties numbered 2,400 that first day, including six hundred killed.

Mount Suribachi fell to the Marines after four days of savage fighting. The Marines captured the rest of the island after inch-by-inch fighting on March 26, at a cost of six thousand dead Marines. Only two hundred Japanese survived.

In perhaps the most famous photograph of World War II, taken by Associated Press photographer Joe Rosenthal, US Marines of the 28th Regiment, 5th Marine Division, raise the American flag atop Mount Suribachi, Iwo Jima, on February 23, 1945.

Questioning the Bomb

In March 1945, General Groves briefed FDR on the Manhattan Project: one of two versions of the A-bomb might be ready for use by late spring 1945. While the fighting still raged on Iwo Jima, Secretary Stimson updated FDR again on the A-bomb development. FDR questioned whether the bomb should actually be dropped or only used as a threat. He would never face that decision.

Scientists assigned to the Manhattan Project worked in secret at the Los Alamos National Laboratory in New Mexico to develop the world's first atomic bomb.

Tragedy Strikes

At home, tragedy struck on April 12. That morning, while vacationing in Warm Springs, Georgia, FDR woke up complaining of a headache. Two hours later, the president was dead. Diagnosis: cerebral hemorrhage.

Senator Robert Taft, a longtime political opponent of Roosevelt, later eloquently summed up his remarkable life: "The President's death removed the greatest figure of our time at the very climax of his career, and shocks the world to which his words and actions were more important than those of any other man. He dies a hero of the war, for he literally worked himself to death in the service of the American people."[5]

The news of FDR's death stunned the American public and citizens of the world, none more so than Vice President Harry S. Truman. The presidency devolved to him. Speaking to the press on April 12, Truman said, "I don't know if any of you fellows ever had a load of hay or a bull fall on him, but last night the whole weight of the moon and stars fell on me. I feel a tremendous responsibility. Please pray for me."[6]

Truman complained about the responsibility forced upon him. "I'm not big enough for the job,"[7] he said. History proved him wrong. In the days ahead, his performance as the nation's thirty-third president would show him to be big enough—with some to spare.

Truman Takes Charge

Truman undertook the big job of the American presidency with little knowledge of his former boss's vision and plans for foreign policy. During his eighty-three days as vice president, he had experienced only limited contact with the president. FDR, perhaps with a false mindset of personal immortality, failed to anticipate his own sudden death. He had felt little compulsion to keep his potential successor informed of his intended strategy for winning the war.

FDR, for example, never told Truman about the ongoing program to build an atomic bomb. Nor did he apprise him of any of the great postwar problems he foresaw in Europe and Asia. Accordingly, Truman was forced to rely on Roosevelt's advisers and on his own wits and instinct to deal with events related to the final phases of the war in Europe.

In his first speech to the nation on April 16, 1945, Truman declared his intention of continuing Roosevelt's policy of demanding the unconditional surrender of Germany and Japan. By affirming the continuance of existing plans, he hoped to assure Americans and their allies of a smooth transition in leadership. Truman stayed true to his word.

In Berlin, Hitler celebrated his fifty-sixth birthday with top Nazis in his *Führerbunker* beneath the Reich Chancellery in Berlin. A week later, on April 27, Italian partisans captured and killed Mussolini and his mistress, Clara Petacci, at the village of Dongo near Lake Como. They trucked their bodies to Milan, kicked and beat them, and then strung them up by their feet in front of a gas station.

Three days later, on April 30, with Allied armies closing like a vise on Berlin from the east and west, Hitler and his newly wedded wife, Eva Braun, committed suicide in Hitler's bunker. Eva took poison; Hitler shot himself. His staff cremated their bodies in the Chancellery garden.

Grim-faced German officers Colonel General Alfred Gustav Jodl and Admiral Hans-Georg von Friedeburg sign the German surrender document at Reims, France, on May 7, 1945.

Berlin fell to advancing Soviet troops on May 2. Germany surrendered unconditionally to the Western Allies in a schoolhouse at Reims on May 7—V-E Day. To symbolize unity among the victors—allegedly—the Soviets repeated the surrender ceremony in Berlin the next day. So ended World War II in Europe.

Across the globe, the conflict with Japan remained a war to be won. The task of finishing it rested heavy on the narrow shoulders of Harry S. Truman.

CHAPTER NINE

ENDGAME IN THE PACIFIC

Germany's surrender failed to mute the fighting fury of 100,000 of General Mitsuru Ushijima's Thirty-Second Japanese Army as defenders dug in on Okinawa. Ushijima and his soldiers viewed the island as Japan's last chance to check the Allied advance in the Pacific and save their homeland from invasion. Their stated creed was: "One plane for one warship. One boat for one ship. One man for ten enemy. One man for one tank."[1] If they had to die for their emperor and homeland, they would not die easy.

Okinawa formed a part of the Ryukyu group, south of the Japanese home islands and Formosa. Allied war planners chose it over the Philippines as the final spring-board to the anticipated invasion of Japan. The assault was code-named Operation Iceberg. It assembled the largest invasion fleet of the Pacific War, second only to that of the Allied landings in Normandy. It consisted of some 1,500 combatant and auxiliary vessels. The British chipped in with a task force of twenty-two ships. They included four

War supplies and military equipment pour ashore from landing craft that dot the sea from shore to horizon, as US invasion forces establish a beachhead on Okinawa island, about 350 miles (560 kilometers) from the Japanese mainland, on April 13, 1945.

carriers with 244 aircraft to add to almost one thousand US aircraft. A half-million men took part in the action.

On the first day, April 1, 1945, two Marine and two Army divisions swarmed ashore—about sixty thousand men—under the command of Army General Simon B. Buckner. Two Marine and one Army divisions were held in reserve. One Marine division deployed northward up the Motobu Peninsula; the other joined the two Army divisions and advanced to the south. Offshore, Allied warships pummeled Japanese positions with naval gunfire and rockets, while under attack by waves of Admiral Matome Ugaki's *kamikazes*—Japanese suicide pilots and aircraft.

Desperate Defenses

On April 6, a seven hundred-plane *kamikaze* attack on the Okinawa invasion fleet inflicted heavy damage on thirteen US destroyers. But the *kamikazes* were not Japan's only suicidal means of mounting a desperate defense. Japan's High Command ordered the remnants of the Japanese Combined Fleet to the waters off Okinawa on a similar suicide mission.

Led by Admiral Seiichi Ito in his flagship, the battleship *Yamato*, accompanied by a light cruiser and eight destroyers put to sea in early April. Their mission—called Operation Ten-Go—was to destroy the US fleet operating off Okinawa. Ito's ships lacked sufficient fuel for a return voyage—hence a true suicide mission.

Aircraft belonging to US Admiral Marc Mitscher's strike force spotted Ito's battle squadron on April 3. Mitscher's pilots struck the Japanese fleet with wave after wave of bombing and torpedo runs, sinking the *Yamato* and several of its escorts within hours. Ito chose to go down with his flagship. Another desperate defense failed.

During the battle for Okinawa, Japanese suicide pilots known as *kamikazes* (Divine Wind) wreaked havoc upon the US invasion fleet in a valiant—but vain—attempt to repulse the American invaders.

Ushijima's defenders fought fanatically, but US Marine and Army attackers persevered grimly. They captured two airfields on the second day. The three divisions in the south reached the Shuri defenses on April 4. Fighting descended into a yard-by-yard advance in some of the bloodiest action of the island campaigns, claiming high casualties.

On May 11, General Buckner—who was later killed in action—ordered a renewed offensive on the Shuri defenses, forcing Ushijima to withdraw. Fighting continued on the island until the last week in June. The victors found General Ushijima and his chief of staff dead. Both had committed *hara-kiri*, the ritual Japanese suicide.

The Battle of Okinawa officially ended on July 2, 1945. In the bloody conflict, almost fifty thousand Americans were killed or wounded. Only a few Japanese survived.

Exceeding Expectations

After Germany's surrender, President Harry S. Truman warmed quickly to his new job as leader of the free world. He immediately recognized the threat of Soviet expansionism. The Soviets' aggressive assertion of their self-interests in eastern Europe—particularly in Poland—angered him. He accused them of breaking the Yalta agreements made with Roosevelt in February 1945. But he felt encouraged by their seeming cooperation at the San Francisco conference in April and May, which established the United Nations (UN).

Hoping to save lives in Asia, Truman pressed the Soviets to join the continuing war against Japan. He also ordered the continuation of the A-bomb project. At Truman's suggestion for a meeting of the Big Three, the Soviets agreed to talks at Potsdam, a Berlin suburb, to discuss Japan and postwar plans from July 17 to August 3.

At Potsdam, after returning from a tour of Berlin's rubbled streets, Truman received a top-secret cable. It stated: "Diagnosis not yet complete but results seem satisfactory and already exceed expectations."[2]

The cable came from General Leslie R. Groves, the military commander of the atom-bomb project at Alamogordo, New Mexico. His message informed Truman of the recent progress of the Manhattan Project. The message bolstered Truman's confidence as he prepared for his first meeting with Soviet Premier Joseph Stalin.

Truman wrote in his diary: "Believe Japs will fold up before Russian [Stalin] comes in."[3] His note referred to Stalin's pledge to join the war against Japan once Germany had been defeated. In February 1945, the Soviet leader had made his vow to FDR and Churchill at the Yalta Conference in Crimea. In return, Stalin was to receive territorial concessions in Asia. Truman intended to honor the Yalta agreements made by FDR.

Illuminating News

Truman's aims at the conference were twofold: (1) to lay a foundation for rebuilding postwar Europe and (2) to solicit Soviet participation in the war against Japan. The meeting began on July 17. Truman, buoyed up by the news from General Groves, took charge of the meeting. As Churchill later recalled, the president "stood up to the Russians in a most emphatic manner."[4] Stalin declared his intention of declaring war on Japan by August 15 at the latest. Truman, elated at first, changed his mind when a second cable from General Groves arrived on July 21.

In his official report, Groves described the successful A-bomb detonation:

> The test was successful beyond the most optimistic expectations of anyone … I estimate the energy generated to be in the excess of the equivalent of 15,000 to 20,000 tons [13,608 to 18,144 metric tons] of TNT … For a brief period there was a lightning effect within a radius of 20 miles [32 km] equal to several suns at midday; a huge ball of fire was formed which lasted for several seconds. This ball mushroomed and rose to a height of over ten thousand feet [3 km] before it dimmed.[5]

With the general's optimistic report in hand, Truman and his advisers then questioned the need for Soviet help in ending the war against Japan. Nor would the United States need to execute its plan to invade Japan at a huge cost of American casualties.

The United States now had a way to end the war quickly without Soviet aid or resorting to a costly invasion of the Japanese home islands. American war planners moved swiftly in an attempt to force Japan's surrender before the Soviets declared war.

Truman decided to alert Stalin to the addition of the bomb to the US arsenal, rather than to risk the resentment of the Soviets when they found out about it later anyway. After the day's conference on July 24, Truman "casually mentions to Stalin that we had a new weapon of unusual destructive force."[6] Stalin, who already knew about the bomb through his spies, replied, almost as casually, that

Downfall

The Allied plan to invade the Japanese home islands—called Operation Downfall—was divided into two main operations: "Olympic" and "Coronet." Olympic called for an assault on Kyushu, the southernmost Japanese island, in the fall of 1945. The Americans planned on using air bases on Kyushu to launch attacks elsewhere in Japan. Coronet, the invasion of the main island of Honshu, was set for March 1946.

War planners selected Kyushu and Honshu because they knew those two islands offered the only beaches large enough to accommodate a huge amphibious operation. They also knew the Japanese were well aware of that and would heavily defend those beaches. Moreover, the suicidal attacks of the *kamikazes* at Okinawa demonstrated the willingness of the Japanese to defend their homeland to the last man, woman, and child.

The US Joint Chiefs of Staff estimated that the invasion of both islands would claim 1.2 million American casualties, including 267,000 dead. Japanese casualties, as projected by the Navy Department, totaled as many as ten million. These figures were only numbers on paper, but they would clearly weigh heavily on any decision to use the atomic bomb.

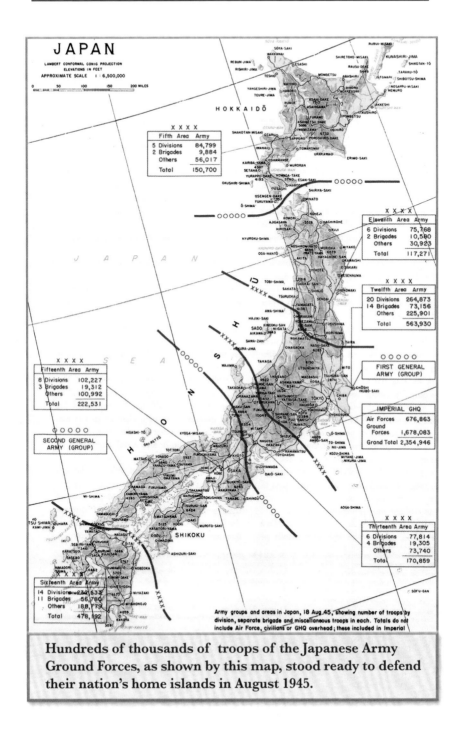

JAPAN

LAMBERT CONFORMAL CONIC PROJECTION
ELEVATIONS IN FEET
APPROXIMATE SCALE 1 : 6,500,000

0   50   100   150   200 MILES

HOKKAIDŌ

X X X X
Fifth Area Army

5 Divisions	84,799
2 Brigades	9,884
Others	56,017
Total	150,700

X X X X
Eleventh Area Army

6 Divisions	75,768
2 Brigades	10,580
Others	30,923
Total	117,271

X X X X
Twelfth Area Army

20 Divisions	264,873
14 Brigades	73,156
Others	225,901
Total	563,930

X X X X
Fifteenth Area Army

8 Divisions	102,227
3 Brigades	19,312
Others	100,992
Total	222,531

FIRST GENERAL ARMY (GROUP)

IMPERIAL GHQ

Air Forces	676,863
Ground Forces	1,678,083
Grand Total	2,354,946

SECOND GENERAL ARMY (GROUP)

HONSHŪ

SHIKOKU

X X X X
Thirteenth Area Army

6 Divisions	77,814
4 Brigades	19,305
Others	73,740
Total	170,859

X X X X
Sixteenth Area Army

14 Divisions	232,653
11 Brigades	56,760
Others	188,779
Total	478,192

Army groups and areas in Japan, 18 Aug 45, showing number of troops by division, separate brigade and miscellaneous troops in each. Totals do not include Air Force, civilians or GHQ overhead; these included in Imperial

Hundreds of thousands of troops of the Japanese Army Ground Forces, as shown by this map, stood ready to defend their nation's home islands in August 1945.

Major General Carl Spaatz, commander of US Strategic Air Forces, directed the strategic bombing of Japan, including the bombing of Hiroshima and Nagasaki.

"he was glad to hear it and hoped we would make good use of it against the Japanese."[7]

Fateful Decision

That same day, Truman approved an order from the Joint Chiefs of Staff to General Carl A. Spaatz, commander of the Strategic Air Forces: "The twentieth Air Force will deliver its first special bomb as soon as weather will permit visual bombing after about August 3, 1945 on one of the targets: Hiroshima, Kokura, Niigata and Nagasaki."[8]

FDR had left behind a legacy of using the atomic bomb militarily against Japan. Although Roosevelt opposed the use of chemical or biological weapons, he had come to consider the A-bomb as simply an escalation of conventional explosives. Now that the atomic weapon had become available, it fell to Truman to act on Roosevelt's intent. General Groves saw Truman's fateful decision to use the bomb against Japan as "one of noninterference—basically a decision not to upset the existing plans."[9]

Two days later, on July 26, the Big Three powers issued the Potsdam Declaration. The edict warned, in part, that Allied forces were positioned for a final assault of imperial Japan. It called upon Japan to surrender unconditionally or face "utter destruction."[10]

CHAPTER TEN

"RAIN OF RUIN"

Japanese leaders received the Potsdam edict. Some Japanese diplomats favored suing for peace, but they could not abide the "unconditional" term in the Allied ultimatum. They feared the Allied demand would depose their emperor, Hirohito. This, in turn, would terminate his centuries-old line of direct descent from the Japanese sun goddess Amaterasu. Japan rejected the Allied terms.

Responding to the rejection, Truman said, "There was no alternative now."[1]

Little Boy

On July 26, 1945, while Japanese leaders argued their next moves, the US heavy cruiser *Indianapolis* arrived at the island of Tinian in the Marianas. Its new captain, Charles Butler McVay, breathed a sigh of relief. His cruiser had just completed a high-speed dash across the Pacific from San Francisco via Pearl Harbor to deliver a mysterious cargo. Its top-secret freight consisted of lead buckets containing

On August 9, 1945, this infamous mushroom cloud rose to 20,000 feet (6,000 meters) above Nagasaki, Japan, symbolizing the enormous destructive power of the atomic bomb. Japan surrendered five days later, on August 14, to end World War II.

Roots of Empire

One of several Japanese foundation legends holds that heaven and earth evolved out of chaos. The birth of several generations of gods followed. The gods went unnamed until the arrival of the god Izanagi (he who invites) and the goddess Izanami (she who invites). Ordered by their heavenly superiors, this divine pair stood on the floating bridge of heaven and stirred the ocean below with a spear. As the water dripped from the point of their withdrawn spear, the droplets solidified to form the eight sacred islands of Japan.

To populate these islands, the gods created a multitude of divine or semi-divine beings, including the sun goddess Amaterasu, leader of the celestial gods (said to have been born from the left eye of her father, Izanagi).

Amaterasu sent her grandson to earth. He married, and the marriage produced the father of Jimmu, the founder and first emperor of Japan. Jimmu reigned from 660 to 585 BCE. His reign—placed in the early Christian era by modern historians—marks the start of an unbroken line of Japanese emperors and empresses. It remains intact today.

Legend has it that sun goddess Amaterasu hid from the world in a cave after her brother insulted her. But, as this painting depicts, she was lured out by other gods dancing and the sounds of their merriment. It is said that her emergence from the cave restored light to the world.

precious uranium-235 charges for the "Little Boy" atomic bomb. Associated fifteen-foot (4.6-km) crates flown in by air carried the bomb's firing gun and casing.

The *Indianapolis* was the former flagship of the US Fifth Fleet. It had been in San Francisco undergoing repairs from a *kamikaze* attack off Okinawa. Its selection for this assignment came purely by chance. Neither McVay nor his crew of more than one thousand men knew what their cargo contained. But the captain knew from his instructions that the contents were of vital importance. His orders said to guard the cargo night and day.

More telling—and more ominous—McVay's orders stressed: "If she [his ship] goes down, save the cargo at all costs, in a lifeboat if necessary. And every day you save on your voyage will cut the length of the war by just as much."[2]

At 2:45 in the early morning of August 6, 1945, a large aircraft taxied into take-off position on the long runway at the Tinian airstrip. It was a Boeing B-29 Superfortress, a four-engine plane capable of long-distance flights. Colonel Paul W. Tibbets, its pilot, had nicknamed the bomber *Enola Gay* after his mother. The name belied the bomber's lethal cargo and destructive mission. Its cargo was Little Boy.

Little Boy's name was misleading as it was not so little. It was ten and a half feet long (3.2 meters) and twenty-nine inches (73.7 centimeters) around, it weighed some 9,700 pounds (4,400 kilograms). Within its blue-steel casing, the bomb held enormous explosive power. Tibbets and twelve others held their breath as the heavily laden bomber roared down the Tinian airstrip. Little Boy remained unarmed. A crash on takeoff with an armed bomb would send them all to eternity and take most of the island with them.

The Last Ship

Despite the swift completion of its mission, the end of the war came too late for the cruiser *Indianapolis* and its crew. With its A-bomb cargo safely delivered, it headed for more action off the Philippine island of Leyte. It never reached its new destination.

On July 30, 1945, the Japanese submarine I-58 sank the cruiser. She sank so fast that there was no time to send out an SOS, the international signal of distress. As a result, only 316 of its more than one thousand officers and men survived. The *Indianapolis* became the last major warship lost during World War II. The loss of the ill-fated cruiser and its men remains one of the US Navy's worst sea disasters.

In one of the US Navy's saddest tragedies, the US heavy cruiser *Indianapolis*, shown steaming smartly here, was sunk by a Japanese submarine after delivering atomic-bomb material to the island of Tinian in the South Pacific. Only 316 crew members survived.

Enola Gay's four engines whined and strained. The silver-skinned B-29 picked up speed and at last left the earth behind. Tibbets set a course for the home islands of Japan.

New Age

The *Enola Gay* and two escorting B-29s of Special Bombing Mission 13 arrived over the Japanese city of Hiroshima at 0814. One minute and seventeen seconds later, *Enola Gay*'s bomb bay doors opened. Little Boy plummeted free. It wobbled a little until it gathered speed in its downward flight. The people of Hiroshima never heard the bomb's supersonic screech. Barometric pressure triggered Little Boy's detonating mechanism at exactly 1,800 feet (549 m). A brief flash expanded in split milliseconds to engulf the city below in a great ball of light and destructive force.

Colonel Tibbets viewed the sight from 30,800 feet (9.4 km) above Hiroshima. He afterward exclaimed, "There was the mushroom cloud growing up, and we watched it blossom. And down below it the thing reminded me more of a boiling pot of tar than any other description I can give it. It was black and boiling with a steam haze on top of it."[3] The "boiling pot of tar" instantly consumed an estimated eighty thousand lives and ultimately as many as 200,000, as the world entered the Atomic Age.

Fat Man

At 1045 that same morning, Washington time, President Truman issued a statement announcing and explaining the bombing. "It was to spare the Japanese people from utter destruction that the ultimatum of July 26 was issued at Potsdam. Their leaders promptly rejected the ultimatum. If they do not now accept our terms, they may expect a rain of ruin from the air the like of which has never been seen on this earth."[4]

The second Allied ultimatum went unheeded in Japan.

Two days after the bombing of Hiroshima, the Soviets declared war on Japan. US military planners then decided to drop a second A-bomb on Japan. They felt it was needed to convince the Japanese of a continuing US capability for mass destruction. The target this time was Nagasaki, a shipbuilding center on the Japanese island of Kyushu.

A second flight of three B-29 Superfortresses arrived over target at 1201 in the afternoon of August 9, 1945. The lead bomber—nicknamed the *Grand Artiste*—carried an atomic bomb codenamed "Fat Man." The bomb's plutonium-charged substance equaled an explosive energy of somewhere between twenty thousand and forty thousand tons (18,144 and 36,287 metric tons) of TNT. About another eighty thousand people died in Nagasaki. Sixty percent of the city disappeared.

That evening, Japanese Emperor Hirohito met with the Supreme Council. He told them of his desire to accept the Potsdam terms, with one exception: he wanted to preserve the imperial institution. The next day, August 10, the Japanese government announced its acceptance of the Potsdam Declaration, provided that "it does not compromise any demand which prejudices the prerogatives of His Majesty as a Sovereign Ruler."[5]

In Washington, the Japanese announcement received mixed reactions. A telegram from one congressman urged strict compliance to Allied demands for an "unconditional surrender." Of 170 telegrams received at the White House in twenty-four hours, 153 echoed the legislator's viewpoint, as did Secretary of State James F. Byrnes. Secretary of War Henry L. Stimson offered a different view. He suggested that allowing the Japanese to retain their emperor might save "us from a score of bloody Iwo Jimas and Okinawas."[6] Only he held the authority to command Japanese forces in Manchuria, China, and Southeast Asia to surrender.

Secretary Byrnes effected a compromise. He drafted a letter in reply to Japan's provisory acceptance of surrender terms. It insisted that the ruling authority of the emperor and the Japanese government would be subject to the discretion of the supreme commander of the Allied powers in effecting the terms of surrender.

Japan's leaders received Byrnes's letter on August 11. After three days of haggling between military hawks and diplomatic doves, the emperor implored his ministers to "bow to my wishes and accept the Allied reply forthwith."[7]

On August 14, 1945, in an imperial rescript (decree), Emperor Hirohito told his subjects: "The enemy has for the first time used cruel bombs to kill and maim extremely large numbers of the innocent, and the heavy casualties are beyond measure. To continue the war further could lead in the end not only to the extermination of our race, but also to the destruction of all human civilization."[8] With that, he announced his acceptance of Allied demands to end the war, in order to "open the way for a great peace for thousands of generations to come."[9]

Hope for a Better World

On September 2, 1945, General Douglas MacArthur presided over a formal surrender ceremony aboard the

Japanese foreign minister Mamoru Shigemitsu looks on as American lieutenant general Richard K. Sutherland signs the surrender document aboard the US battleship *Missouri* on September 2, 1945.

US battleship *Missouri* in Tokyo Bay. Japanese and Allied representatives signed the surrender document. MacArthur concluded the ceremony, saying:

> It is my earnest hope, indeed the hope of all mankind, that from this solemn occasion a better world shall emerge out of the blood and carnage of the past ... a world dedicated to the dignity of man ... Let us pray that peace be now restored to the world, and that God will preserve it always. These proceedings are closed.[10]

After six tumultuous years of grim theater on a global stage, the curtain finally came down on World War II.

CONCLUSION

Franklin Delano Roosevelt aspired to high office and achieved it with his election as the nation's thirty-second president in 1932. He took the helm of the ship of state during the Great Depression. His policies—particularly those of the New Deal—helped to guide the nation with a steady hand through a collapsed economy. And his warm and friendly voice during regular Fireside Chats offered assurance to millions of Americans that happy days would surely come again for all of them. FDR's positive leadership earned him reelection in 1936, 1940, and 1944—the only American president to win a third and fourth term.

During his second term, war broke out in Europe with the advent of Fascist dictators Adolf Hitler, Benito Mussolini, and Francisco Franco. FDR walked a thin line of flexible neutrality, skillfully maneuvering to assist war-torn Britain across the Atlantic, while containing an increasingly aggressive Japan beyond the Pacific. Envisioning the day when America would inevitably be drawn into the war, he vigorously shepherded an unprecedented

President Franklin Delano Roosevelt in his prime, sporting a dapper bow tie and a warm, engaging smile.

buildup of American arms and armed forces.

Acting always in what he considered to be the best interests of the American people, FDR even resorted to deceiving the public to ensure its safety. He recognized that if Germany defeated Britain, which stood alone against the powerful Nazi war machine, Germany would become dominant on the European continent and in the Atlantic Ocean. Accordingly, he prepared America for war—against the protests of isolationists—while assuring all Americans that he would keep the United States out of the European war.

Within months of his reelection in 1940, FDR devised the Lend-Lease plan and secured its passage in Congress, still assuring Americans that he would send none of their boys off to war. Passage of the Lend-Lease Act firmly linked the American economy to the long-term support of its future European allies. When Japan attacked Pearl Harbor on December 7, 1941, isolationist protests vanished in a heartbeat, along with all opposition to British support.

Months before the United States entered the war, FDR forged an alliance with Winston Churchill. Together, they issued the Atlantic Charter, which in its tenets established their vision for the postwar world. As one of the Big Three leaders of the alliance against Hitler and his allies, FDR took on an international role. He recognized that both Stalin and Churchill held different views of a world without war. Though criticized for his concessions to Stalin at Yalta, he tiptoed through their differences and held to a steady course that resulted in victory.

At home, FDR oversaw a massive growth in the American economy and built its armed forces into a fighting force unparalleled then or now. He authorized the development of the A-bomb, though it fell to his successor to assign the time and place of its use. His wartime efforts directly contributed to the status of the United States as today's only superpower. Second only to Abraham Lincoln, history will likely regard Franklin Delano Roosevelt as the most important president of the twentieth century.

CHRONOLOGY

1882

Franklin Delano Roosevelt is born in Hyde Park, New York.

1922

Benito Mussolini becomes dictator of Italy.

1932

Roosevelt elected president of the United States.

1933

Adolf Hitler is named chancellor of Germany.

1935

Italy invades Abyssinia. Congress passes the Neutrality Act.

1936

Hitler and Mussolini form an alliance.

1937

Roosevelt is elected to a second term. Sino-Japanese War begins.

1940

Roosevelt is elected to a third term. Tripartite Pact creates the Berlin-Rome-Tokyo Axis.

1941

June 22
Germany invades the Soviet Union.

December 7
Japan attacks Pearl Harbor on Oahu, Hawaii.

December 8
United States declares war on Japan.

December 11
Germany and Italy declare war on the United States.

1942

June 4-7
US Navy defeats Japanese fleet at Midway.

August 7
US Marines and soldiers invade Guadalcanal.

November 8
Operation Torch in North Africa begins.

1943

July 10
Anglo-American forces invade Sicily in Operation Husky.

September 3
Allies invade Italy.

September 8
Italy surrenders.

November 20-24
US Marines capture Tarawa in the Gilbert Islands.

November 28-December 1
Roosevelt and Churchill meet with Joseph Stalin at Tehran Conference.

1944

June 6
Allies land in Normandy.

June 15
US Marines and soldiers invade Saipan in the Marianas.

December 16
Battle of the Bulge; battle ends January 28, 1945.

1945

February 4-11
Roosevelt, Churchill, and Stalin meet at Yalta in Crimea.

February 19-March 26
US Marines and soldiers capture Iwo Jima

March 9-10
US bombs Tokyo.

April 1-July 2
US defeats Japanese on Okinawa in the Ryukyu Islands.

April 12
Roosevelt dies. Harry S. Truman becomes president.

April 27
Mussolini and his mistress are killed.

April 30
Hitler and Eva Braun commit suicide.

May 7
Germany surrenders. World War II in Europe ends.

July 17-August 2
Truman meets with Churchill and Stalin at the Potsdam Conference.

August 6
US bomber *Enola Gay* drops A-bomb on Hiroshima.

August 9
US bomber *Grand Artiste* drops A-bomb on Nagasaki.

August 15
Japan accepts unconditional surrender terms.

September 2
World War II ends.

CHAPTER NOTES

INTRODUCTION

1. Jean Edward Smith, *FDR* (New York: Random House, 2007), p. 302.

CHAPTER 1: DATE OF INFAMY

1. John Costello, *The Pacific War* (New York: Quill, 1982), p. 119.
2. Gordon W. Prange, with Donald L. Goldstein and Katherine V. Dillon, *At Dawn We Slept: The Untold Story of Pearl Harbor* (New York: McGraw-Hill, 1981), p. 445.
3. Ibid., p. 472.
4. Mitsuo Fuchida and Masatake Okumiya, *Midway: The Battle That Doomed Japan, the Japanese Navy's Story* (Annapolis, MD: Naval Institute Press, 1992), p. 50.
5. Costello, p. 130.
6. Mitsuo Fuchida, "I Led the Attack on Pearl Harbor," in Reader's Digest Association. *Reader's Digest Illustrated History of World War II* (Pleasantville, NY: Reader's Digest Association, 1978), p. 19.
7. Martin Gilbert, *The Second World War: A Complete History* (New York: Henry Holt & Company, 1989), p. 272.
8. Nigel Hamilton, *The Mantle of Command: FDR at War, 1941–1942* (Boston: Mariner Books, 2014), pp. 76–77.

CHAPTER 2: PATH TOWARD DISASTER

1. Williamson Murray and Allan R. Millett, *A War to Be Won: Fighting the Second World War* (Cambridge, MA: Belnap Press of Harvard University Press, 2000), p. 4.
2. C. L. Sulzberger, *World War II*, The American Heritage Library (New York: American Heritage Press, 1985), p. 18.
3. H. W. Brands, *Traitor to His Class: The Privileged Life and Radical Presidency of Franklin Delano Roosevelt* (New York: Anchor Books, 2008), p. 481.
4. Ibid., p. 446.
5. Ibid.
6. Ibid.

CHAPTER 3: THE WINDS OF WAR

1. H. W. Brands, *Traitor to His Class: The Privileged Life and Radical Presidency of Franklin Delano Roosevelt* (New York: Anchor Books, 2008), p. 496.

2. Robert Leckie, *The Wars of America*, Vol. II (New York: Harper-Perennial, 1992), p. 681.
3. Jean Edward Smith, *FDR* (New York: Random House, 2007), p. 423.
4. Ibid.
5. Ibid.
6. Ibid., p. 424.
7. Brands, p. 509.
8. Leckie, p. 682.
9. Louis L. Snyder, *Encyclopedia of the Third Reich* (New York: Paragon House Publishers, 1989), p. 298.

CHAPTER 4: AMERICA'S UNDECLARED WAR

1. Norman Polmar and Thomas B. Allen, *World War II: The Encyclopedia of the War Years 1941–1945* (New York: Random House, 1996), p. 144.
2. Jean Edward Smith, *FDR* (New York: Random House, 2007), p. 511.
3. H. W. Brands, *Traitor to His Class: The Privileged Life and Radical Presidency of Franklin Delano Roosevelt* (New York: Anchor Books, 2008), p. 574.
4. Eugene Lyons, "America on the Brink of War," in Reader's Digest Association, *Reader's Digest Illustrated History of World War II* (Pleasantville, NY: Reader's Digest Association, 1978), p. 38.
5. James MacGregor Burns, *Roosevelt 1941–1945: The Soldier of Freedom* (San Diego: Harcourt, 1970), p. 28.
6. Thomas Fleming, *The New Dealers' War: Franklin D. Roosevelt and the War Within World War II* (New York: Basic Books, 2001), p. 89.
7. Joseph E. Persico, *Roosevelt's Centurions: FDR and the Commanders He Led to Victory in World War II* (New York: Random House, 2013), p. 254.

CHAPTER 5: AMERICA JOINS THE FIGHT

1. Maurice Matloff, ed., *American Military History*, Vol. 2, 1902–1996 (Conshohocken, PA: Combined Books, 1996), p. 82.
2. Joseph E. Persico, *Roosevelt's Centurions: FDR and the Commanders He Led to Victory in World War II* (New York: Random House, 2013), p. 121.

3. Norman Polmar and Thomas B. Allen, *World War II: The Encyclopedia of the War Years 1941–1945* (New York: Random House, 1996), p. 226.

4. Persico, p. 254.

5. Nigel Hamilton, *The Mantle of Command: FDR at War, 1941–1942* (Boston: Mariner Books, 2014), p. 284.

6. James MacGregor Burns, *Roosevelt 1941–1945: The Soldier of Freedom* (San Diego: Harcourt, 1970), p. 285.

7. Norman Gelb, "North Africa Campaign," in *The Oxford Companion to American Military History*, edited by John Whiteclay Chambers II (New York: Oxford University Press, 1999), p. 506.

8. Persico, p. 259.

9. Ibid., p. 309.

10. H. W. Brands, *Traitor to His Class: The Privileged Life and Radical Presidency of Franklin Delano Roosevelt* (New York: Anchor Books, 2008), p. 725.

CHAPTER 6: A WORLD AT WAR

1. Jean Edward Smith, *FDR* (New York: Random House, 2007), p. 587.

2. Norman Polmar and Thomas B. Allen, *World War II: The Encyclopedia of the War Years 1941–1945* (New York: Random House, 1996), p. 798.

3. Joseph E. Persico, *Roosevelt's Centurions: FDR and the Commanders He Led to Victory in World War II* (New York: Random House, 2013), p. 343.

4. John Costello, *The Pacific War* (New York: Quill, 1982), p. 431.

5. Polmar and Allen, p. 795.

6. Costello, p. 428.

7. Ibid., p. 438.

8. Persico, p. 393.

9. Costello, p. 474.

10. Michael Haskew, ed., with the Eisenhower Center for American Studies, *The World War II Desk Reference*, Director Douglas Brinkley (New York: HarperResource, 2004), p. 201.

11. H. W. Brands, *Traitor to His Class: The Privileged Life and Radical Presidency of Franklin Delano Roosevelt* (New York: Anchor Books, 2008), p. 763.

CHAPTER 7: **TURNING THE TIDE**

1. Robert Leckie, *The Wars of America*, vol. II (New York: HarperPerennial, 1992), pp. 795–796.
2. Doris Kearns Goodwin, *No Ordinary Time: Franklin & Eleanor Roosevelt: The Home Front in World War II* (New York: Simon & Schuster, 1994), p. 508.
3. Leckie, p. 797.
4. James MacGregor Burns, *Roosevelt 1941–1945: The Soldier of Freedom* (San Diego: Harcourt, 1970), p. 476.
5. H. W. Brands, *Traitor to His Class: The Privileged Life and Radical Presidency of Franklin Delano Roosevelt* (New York: Anchor Books, 2008), p. 774.
6. Ibid.
7. Joseph E. Persico, *Roosevelt's Centurions: FDR and the Commanders He Led to Victory in World War II* (New York: Random House, 2013), p. 391.
8. Burns, p. 527.

CHAPTER 8: **TRIUMPH AND TRAGEDY**

1. Elizabeth-Anne Wheal, Stephen Pope, and James Taylor, *Encyclopedia of the Second World War* (Edison, NJ: Castle Books, 1989), p. 50.
2. Doris Kearns Goodwin, *No Ordinary Time: Franklin & Eleanor Roosevelt: The Home Front in World War II* (New York: Simon & Schuster, 1994), p. 585.
3. Joseph E. Persico, *Roosevelt's Centurions: FDR and the Commanders He Led to Victory in World War II* (New York: Random House, 2013), p. 470.
4. Ibid.
5. Jean Edward Smith, *FDR* (New York: Random House, 2007), p. 636.
6. Robert Leckie, *The Wars of America*, vol. II (New York: HarperPerennial, 1992), p. 820.
7. John Costello, *The Pacific War* (New York: Quill, 1982), p. 567.

CHAPTER 9: **ENDGAME IN THE PACIFIC**

1. Norman Polmar and Thomas B. Allen, *World War II: The Encyclopedia of the War Years 1941–1945* (New York: Random House, 1996), p. 602.

2. John Costello, *The Pacific War* (New York: Quill, 1982), p. 583.
3. Polmar and Allen, p. 654.
4. Ronald H. Spector, *Eagle Against the Sun* (New York: Free Press, 1985), p. 552.
5. Charles L. Mee, Jr., *Meeting at Potsdam* (New York: Franklin Square Press, 1975), pp. 120–121.
6. Polmar and Allen, p. 654.
7. Spector, p. 553.
8. Costello, p. 586.
9. Ibid.
10. Michael Haskew, ed., with the Eisenhower Center for American Studies, *The World War II Desk Reference*, director Douglas Brinkley (New York: HarperResource, 2004), p. 153.

CHAPTER 10: "RAIN OF RUIN"

1. John Costello, *The Pacific War* (New York: Quill, 1982), p. 588.
2. Ibid., p. 587.
3. Michael Haskew, ed., with the Eisenhower Center for American Studies, *The World War II Desk Reference*, director Douglas Brinkley (New York: HarperResource, 2004), p. 298.
4. Douglas Brinkley, general ed., *World War II: The Allied Counteroffensive, 1942–1945*, *The New York Times* Living History Series, edited by David Rubel (New York: Times Books, Henry Holt and Co., 2003), p. 362.
5. Ronald H. Spector, *Eagle Against the Sun* (New York: Free Press, 1985), p. 556.
6. Ibid.
7. Ibid., p. 557.
8. John W. Dower, *Embracing Defeat: Japan in the Wake of World War II* (New York: W. W. Norton and Co., 1997), p. 36.
9. Ibid.
10. Haskew, p. 498.

GLOSSARY

alliance A union or association formed for mutual benefit, especially of countries by treaty.

army A large military unit consisting of a headquarters, two or more corps, and auxiliary units.

atrocity A wicked or cruel act.

attrition A gradual wearing down of strength and morale.

battalion A military unit made up of several companies that forms a part of a regiment.

celebratory A festive manner.

commodity A useful thing, such as an article of trade or a product.

consign To hand over or deliver formally.

corps A military unit consisting of two or more divisions and auxiliary arms and services.

division A major military unit made up of several regiments.

emissary A person sent to conduct negotiations.

Fascist One who subscribes to a system of extreme right-wing dictatorial government.

grandiose Something imposing or planned on a large scale.

inexorably Relentlessly; unable to be deterred.

isolationism A policy of holding aloof from other countries by refraining from alliances and other international political and economic relations.

neutrality The policy or status of a nation that does not participate in war.

quarantine To place in a state of enforced isolation.

regiment A military unit of ground forces consisting of two or more battalions.

reparation Compensation for war damage, demanded by the victor of a defeated enemy.

superstructure A structure that rests on something else, such as a structure above deck on a ship.

FURTHER READING

BOOKS

Bolden, Tonya. *FDR's Alphabet Soup: New Deal America 1932–1939*. New York: Knopf Books for Young Readers, 2010.

Grayson, Robert. *Roosevelts*. America's Great Political Families Series. Edina, MN: Essential Library (Abdo Publishing), 2016.

Marrin, Albert. *Uprooted: The Japanese Experience During World War II*. New York: Knopf Books for Young Readers, 2016.

———. *FDR and the American Crisis*. New York: Knopf Books for Young Readers, 2015.

Thompson, Ben. *Guts & Glory: World War II*. Boston: Little, Brown Books for Young Readers, 2016.

WEBSITES

FDR Presidential Library & Museum
fdrlibrary.org/resources-for-students
A visual depiction of players and events for students

Franklin D. Roosevelt Biography
www.biography.com/people/franklin-d-roosevelt-9463381
Highlights of FDR's life

World War II: Everything You Need
www.scholastic.com/teachers/unit/world-war-ii
Eyewitness interviews, lesson plans, and other resources help students discover the history of World War II and the conflict's lasting impact

FILMS

American Experience: FDR
Directed by David Grubin. PBS, 1988.

Great Americans: Franklin D. Roosevelt
Smith Show Media Group Inc., 2016

INDEX

A

Allies, 39, 54, 59, 62, 66, 70, 71, 73, 75, 78, 84, 88, 93
American neutrality, 7, 25, 27, 28, 39, 46, 50, 113
atom bomb, 51, 57, 62, 90, 97, 99
Atomic Age, 109
Axis powers, 23, 40, 52, 60, 62, 72

B

Betio, 66, 67
Big Three, 63–64, 97, 103, 115
Bulge, Battle of the, 84–86

C

Cairo Conference, 63
"cash and carry," 29, 35
Chamberlain, Neville, 37, 38, 39, 40
China, 27, 30, 33, 35, 38, 54, 63, 69, 111
    war in, 30–31
Churchill, Winston, 7, 21, 38, 42, 44, 46, 47, 49, 52, 54, 59, 60, 62, 63, 64, 65, 71, 75, 81, 86, 98, 114

D

D-Day, 73, 74, 78

E

Einstein, Albert, 41

Eisenhower, General Dwight D. ("Ike"), 59, 65, 73, 74, 75, 86, 88
Enola Gay, 107, 109

F

fascism, 21, 23, 25, 27, 29, 30, 113
Fat Man (atomic bomb), 109–111
Franco, General Francisco, 24, 25, 113

G

Germany, 7, 17, 19, 21, 25, 27, 34, 36–37, 39, 41, 44, 52, 60, 64, 75, 78, 81, 86, 92, 98, 114
    arming of, 21
    as Axis power, 40
    declared war, 18
    resigned League of Nations, 21
    surrender, 93, 94, 97
Great Depression, 6, 25, 113

H

Hirohito, Emperor, 104, 110, 111
Hiroshima, 103, 109, 110
Hitler, Adolf, 19, 21, 22, 23, 24, 36, 37, 39, 40, 42, 48, 49, 54, 60, 75, 78, 79, 83, 84, 92, 113, 115
Hopkins, Harry, 44, 47

I

island assaults, 65–66, 68, 70
isolationists, 27, 28, 30, 33, 35, 39, 114
Italy, 18, 21, 23, 24, 25, 34, 38, 39, 44, 62, 71
  as Axis power, 40
  declared war, 18
Iwo Jima, Battle for, 89

J

Japan, 7, 8, 11, 16, 17, 25, 27, 30, 33, 34, 44, 46, 50, 51, 57, 63, 66, 81, 87, 89, 92, 93, 94, 97, 98, 99, 100, 103, 104, 109, 110, 111, 113, 114
  accepts Potsdam, 110–111
  roots of empire, 106
Japanese internment, 55

K

kamikazes, 95, 96, 100, 107
Kursk, Battle of, 61

L

Lend-Lease, 46–47, 49, 54, 114
Little Boy (atomic bomb), 104, 107, 109

M

MacArthur, General Douglas, 56, 66, 68, 70, 78, 80, 82, 111, 112
Manhattan Project, 57, 90, 98
Mussolini, Benito, 21, 23, 25, 30, 40, 92, 113

N

Nagasaki, 103, 110
Neutrality Acts of 1930s, 27, 28–29
New Deal, 6, 113
Normandy, France, 62, 64, 74, 75, 78, 81, 94
nuclear bomb, 41

O

Okinawa, Battle of, 97
operations of WWII, 48, 59, 60, 62, 64, 65, 71, 73, 77, 78, 94, 100

P

Patton, General George S., 59, 60, 81, 85, 88
Pearl Harbor, 8, 11–15, 16, 51, 52, 55, 57, 78, 80, 104
Poland, 41, 42, 88, 97
Potsdam, 98, 103, 109, 110
  Declaration, 103, 104

R

Rape of Nanking, 33
Rommel, Field Marshal Erwin, 60, 75, 77
Roosevelt, Anna Eleanor (wife), 5
Roosevelt, Franklin Delano (FDR), 25, 26, 28, 37, 39, 72, 78, 113
  Arcadia conference, 54
  authorizes exploratory program (atom bomb), 41
  birth, 5

death, 91
declares war, 16–19
education, 5
elected president, 6, 19, 46, 79, 83, 113
extended security, 49
family, 5
Fireside Chats, 47, 72, 113
Four Freedoms, 49
as governor, 6
ill health, 60, 65, 78, 80, 83, 86
legacy, 113–115
marriage, 5
meets with physicists, 51
message to Japanese, 33
policy, 46, 50–51
in public service, 6
readies nation, 44
recognizes Hitler needs to be stopped, 40–41
in Senate, 6
speech on quarantine, 34–35

S
Second New Deal, 6
Soviet-German Nonaggression Pact, 41, 48
Spain, 21, 24, 25
civil war, 24–25, 29
Stalin, Joseph, 7, 25, 59, 60, 63, 64, 65, 86, 88, 98, 99, 115
Stimson, Henry, 44, 46, 57, 59, 90, 111

T
Tehran Conference, 63–64, 97, 103, 115
Tripartite Pact, 44, 46
Truman, Harry S., 79, 91, 93
ordered bombing, 103, 104, 109
as president, 91, 92, 97, 98, 99

U
United Nations, 49, 54, 87, 97
US Pacific Fleet, 11, 14, 15, 52

W
World War II, 8, 22, 33, 50, 55, 84, 93, 112
Allied ultimatum, 110
American heroism, 85
bombing Japan, 88
German surrender, 94
Japanese surrender, 111, 112
last ship, 108
"the longest day," 77
rolling back the enemy, 80–81
sea battles, 82
Soviet aggression, 97

Y
Yalta Conference, 86–87, 88, 97, 98, 115
Declaration on Liberated Europe, 87–88
Yamamoto, Admiral Isoroku, 9, 11, 12